INTRODUCTION TO
NATURAL
LANGUAGE
PROCESSING

INTRODUCTION TO
NATURAL
LANGUAGE
PROCESSING

A PRACTICAL GUIDE FOR BEGINNERS

SAKIL ANSARI

White Falcon
Publishing

www.whitefalconpublishing.com

Introduction to Natural Language Processing
A practical guide for beginners
Sakil Ansari

www.whitefalconpublishing.com

The contents of this book have been certified and timestamped on the
Gnosis blockchain as a permanent proof of existence. Scan the
QR code or visit the URL given on the back cover to
verify the blockchain certification for this book.

ISBN - 978-1-63640-835-4

Dedicated to

My parents, teachers, and friends

PREFACE

Welcome to "**Introduction to Natural Language Processing: A practical guide for beginners**." As the use of computers and technology continues to grow and expand, the ability to communicate with machines using natural language becomes increasingly important. Natural Language Processing (NLP) is the field that deals with this interaction, and it has the potential to revolutionize the way we interact with technology.

This book aims to provide a comprehensive introduction to NLP for beginners. We will start with an overview of NLP and its applications. It is a crucial foundation for NLP, as it helps us understand how language works and how to model it computationally.

Next, we will delve into NLP's different approaches and techniques. This will include syntactic and semantic analysis, which involves analyzing the structure and meaning of words and sentences in a text. The syntactic analysis focuses on the rules of grammar and the relationships between words. In contrast, semantic analysis involves determining the meaning of words and how they relate to each other in a given context.

Another important aspect of NLP is machine translation, which automatically translates text or speech from one language to another. This is a challenging task, as it requires understanding the meanings of words and phrases and taking into account the cultural and contextual differences between languages.

Text classification is another common application of NLP, which involves categorizing text into predefined classes or categories. This can be useful for many tasks, such as sentiment analysis, spam detection, and topic modelling.

Throughout the book, we will provide practical examples to help you apply the concepts and techniques you have learned. We have designed this book to be accessible to beginners, so no prior knowledge of NLP is required.

This book will provide a strong foundation in NLP and inspire you to explore more advanced topics in the field. As the use of computers and technology continues to grow, the demand for professional expertise in NLP is also rising. This book is an excellent starting point for anyone interested in pursuing a career in this exciting and rapidly evolving field.

ACKNOWLEDGEMENT

I want to express my deepest gratitude to everyone who supported me throughout the writing process of this book.

I would also like to thank my editors for their invaluable guidance and input. Their keen eye and expertise helped to shape the book into its final form.

Furthermore, I would like to acknowledge the work of the various researchers and authors I have referenced in this book. Their contributions have greatly enhanced my understanding of the subject matter, which has been essential to the development of the book.

I wholeheartedly thank my professor, Dr V Kamakshi Prasad. He spent his valuable time explaining various complex concepts and always encouraged me.

I want to thank my dad, Alam Ansari Aimar; my mom, Saida Khatun; my brother, Md Haidar Ali Ansari; my sisters, Sakila Khatun and Reehana Khatun and all of my friends and colleagues for their unwavering love and encouragement. Their belief in me and my abilities kept me going when it got tough.

I would like to thank my friend, Chandani Khatun, for her unwavering support throughout the writing of this book. Her encouragement and belief in me meant the world; I couldn't have done it without her. I am forever grateful for her love and support.

Socrates said, "There is no possession more valuable than a good and faithful friend."

I would like to express my gratitude to my dear friend, Rohan Raut. He has been my constant support and inspiration for almost a decade.

Finally, thank my readers for their interest and support. I hope that this book will be of value to them.

Sakil Ansari

CONTENTS

1. Introduction to NLP: What it is and why it matters..........................1
   - Overview of NLP and its applications *1*
   - Types of NLP tasks and techniques *2*
   - Challenges and limitations of NLP *3*

2. Language Basics: Understanding text data and preprocessing techniques........4
   - Tokenization *4*
   - Stemming and lemmatization *6*
   - Stop word removal *7*
   - Case conversion and punctuation removal *8*

3. Exploring Text Data: Tools and techniques for analysing text......................10
   - Descriptive statistics *10*
   - Visualizations *11*
   - Word frequencies and collocations *14*
   - Part-of-speech tagging *15*
   - Named entity recognition *17*

4. Representing Text Data: Techniques for converting text
   into numerical formats 19
   - One-hot encoding *19*
   - Bag-of-words and n-grams *20*
   - Word2vec *23*

5. Classification and Clustering: Organizing text data into categories 25
   - Introduction to classification and clustering *25*
   - Supervised and unsupervised learning *26*
   - Evaluation metrics for classification and clustering *27*
   - Example classification and clustering algorithms *28*

6. Sequence Analysis: Working with sequential data in NLP.............................32
   - Working with sequential data in NLP *32*
   - Sequence tagging *33*
   - Named entity recognition *34*
   - Part-of-speech tagging *35*

7. **Text Generation: Creating text using machine learning techniques** 37

- Introduction to text generation *37*
- Language models and sequence-to-sequence models *37*
- Text generation applications and challenges *39*

8. **Language Translation: Translating the text from one language to another** 42

- Introduction to machine translation *42*
- Translation models and techniques *43*
- Evaluation metrics for translation *44*

9. **Information Extraction: Extracting structured data from unstructured text** 48

- Introduction to information extraction *48*
- Relation extraction *49*
- Event extraction *51*
- Named entity recognition *53*

10. **Text Summarization: Creating concise summaries of text data** 56

- Extractive and abstractive summarization *57*
- Extractive summarization *57*
- Abstractive summarization *58*
- Evaluation metrics for summarization *59*

11. **Sentiment Analysis: Identifying and analysing emotions in text data** 63

- Introduction to sentiment analysis *63*
- Sentiment lexicons and machine learning approaches *64*
- Evaluation metrics for sentiment analysis *68*

12. **Advanced NLP Techniques: Deep learning and beyond** 72

- Introduction to deep learning in NLP *72*
- Popular deep learning models for NLP *73*
- Advanced NLP applications and future directions *77*

13. **Real-World Examples** 80

- Chatbot Implementation Using GPT-3 *80*
- Fake news detection *82*
- Topic modeling *84*
- Article generation using advance NLP *85*
- Semantic-based search *87*
- Autocomplete using NLP *88*

Closing Thoughts 90

Introduction to NLP: What it is and why it matters

## CHAPTER 1

Overview of NLP and its applications

Natural language processing, or NLP, is a fascinating and rapidly growing field of computer science that focuses on the interaction between humans and computers through the use of natural language. At its core, NLP involves the development of algorithms and models that are able to analyze, understand, and generate human language. It involves the development of algorithms and models that can analyze, understand, and generate human language.

One of the primary goals of NLP is to enable computers to better understand and process human language, which has numerous practical applications in a wide range of industries. For example, in healthcare, NLP is used to extract important information from medical records and improve diagnosis and treatment plans. It is also used in finance to analyze customer sentiment and predict stock prices and in customer service to build chatbots that can handle customer inquiries and complaints in a more efficient and personalized way.

In addition to these practical applications, NLP is important because it helps to bridge the gap between humans and computers. It allows us to communicate with computers in a more natural and intuitive way and helps computers to better understand and process human language. As the use of NLP continues to grow, it has the potential to revolutionize how we interact with computers and how we use language in our daily lives. Whether through language translation, sentiment analysis, or chatbots, NLP is an essential tool shaping the future of human-computer interaction.

Overall, NLP is a rapidly growing field with a wide range of applications and the potential to revolutionize how we interact with computers and use language in our daily lives.

Types of NLP tasks and techniques

There are various types of natural language processing (NLP) tasks and techniques that can be used to analyse, understand and generate human language. These tasks and techniques play a crucial role in the field of NLP and can be used in a variety of applications, including language translation, sentiment analysis, and chatbots.

Some common NLP tasks include:

1. **Language translation:** This involves translating text or speech from one language to another. This task is important for businesses and organizations that operate globally and need to communicate with customers and clients in different languages. Language translation can be done using rule-based systems, machine learning algorithms, or deep learning models.
2. **Part-of-speech tagging:** This involves identifying the part of speech (e.g. noun, verb, adjective) of each word in a sentence. Part-of-speech tagging is important for understanding the structure and meaning of a sentence and can be used in tasks such as text summarization and sentiment analysis.
3. **Named entity recognition:** This involves identifying and classifying named entities (e.g. people, organizations, locations) in a text. Named entity recognition is useful for extracting important information from texts and can be used in tasks such as information extraction and question-answering.
4. **Sentiment analysis:** This involves determining the sentiment (e.g. positive, negative, neutral) of a text or speech. Sentiment analysis is useful for businesses and organizations that want to understand how customers feel about their products or services. It can also be used to predict stock prices or election results.
5. **Text Summarization:** This involves creating a shorter version of a text that retains the important information. Text summarization is useful for quickly extracting key points from a long document and can be used in tasks such as information retrieval and summarization of news articles.

There are also various techniques used in NLP, such as:

1. **Rule-based systems:** These use a set of rules to process language. Rule-based systems are simple and easy to understand, but they can be limited in their ability to handle complex language and adapt to new situations.
2. **Machine learning:** These use algorithms to learn from data and make predictions. Machine learning is more flexible and powerful than rule-based systems, but it requires a large amount of data to train on.

3. **Deep learning:** These use artificial neural networks to learn patterns in data. Deep learning is a type of machine learning that has proven to be very effective in tasks such as language translation and image recognition.
4. **Semantic analysis:** This involves analyzing the meaning of words and phrases in a text. Semantic analysis is important for understanding the context and intent of a text and can be used in tasks such as question answering and text classification.

NLP tasks and techniques are an essential part of the field of natural language processing. They allow us to analyze, understand, and generate human language in a variety of applications, and they have the potential to revolutionize how we interact with computers and use language in our daily lives.

Challenges and limitations of NLP

Natural language processing (NLP) has made significant progress in recent years, but it still faces many challenges and limitations. Some of the main challenges and limitations of NLP include the following:

1. **Ambiguity and context:** Human language is often ambiguous and context-dependent, which makes it difficult for computers to accurately interpret and understand it. For example, a word can have multiple meanings depending on the context in which it is used, and the same sentence can have different interpretations depending on the speaker's tone or intent.
2. **Language variability:** Human language varies greatly across different regions, cultures, and dialects. This makes it difficult for NLP systems to accurately process language from different sources.
3. **Lack of annotated data:** Training machine learning models for NLP tasks requires large amounts of annotated data, which can be difficult and time-consuming to obtain. This limits the ability of NLP systems to learn from data and adapt to new situations.
4. **Ethical concerns:** NLP systems can sometimes perpetuate biases and stereotypes present in the data they are trained on. This can have negative consequences, such as when a language translation system translates a sexist phrase or when a sentiment analysis system misinterprets the sentiment of a text.

Despite these challenges and limitations, NLP has made significant progress in recent years and continues to be a rapidly growing field with a wide range of applications. There are ongoing efforts to improve the accuracy and adaptability of NLP systems and address ethical concerns, and it is likely that these systems will continue to evolve and improve in the future.

Language Basics: Understanding text data and preprocessing techniques

Introduction

Text data refers to any data that consists of words, sentences, and paragraphs. This can include things like social media posts, news articles, emails, and more. Text data is usually represented as a sequence of characters, with each character being stored as a string in a computer. One of the unique characteristics of text data is that it is highly unstructured. This means that it is difficult to analyze and understand without some sort of preprocessing or organization. For example, a piece of text may contain misspellings, punctuation errors, or words that are used in different ways (e.g., "run" as a verb or noun). In order to make sense of this data and use it for machine learning tasks, we need to apply some preprocessing techniques to clean and structure the data.

Tokenization

Tokenization is the process of dividing a piece of text into smaller units called tokens. These tokens can be words, phrases, or even individual characters. Tokenization is a fundamental step in natural language processing (NLP) and is used to prepare text data for further analysis.

In Python, there are various libraries and methods that can be used for tokenization. For example, the Natural Language Toolkit (NLTK) library provides several tokenization functions, including word_tokenize and sent_tokenize. Here's an example of how to use these functions:

```
import nltk

# Tokenize a piece of text into words
text = "This is a piece of text that we want to tokenize."
tokens = nltk.word_tokenize(text)
print(tokens)

# Tokenize a piece of text into sentences
text = "This is a piece of text. It has two sentences."
tokens = nltk.sent_tokenize(text)
print(tokens)
```

The output of this code would be:

```
['This', 'is', 'a', 'piece', 'of', 'text', 'that', 'we', 'want', 'to', 'tokenize', '.']

['This is a piece of text.', 'It has two sentences.']
```

Another option is to use the **split()** method, which can be used to split a string into a list of tokens based on a specified delimiter. For example:

```
# Tokenize a piece of text into words
text = "This is a piece of text that we want to tokenize."
tokens = text.split(" ")
print(tokens)

# Tokenize a piece of text into sentences
text = "This is a piece of text. It has two sentences."
tokens = text.split(".")
print(tokens)
```

The output of this code would be:

```
['This', 'is', 'a', 'piece', 'of', 'text', 'that', 'we', 'want', 'to', 'tokenize.']

['This is a piece of text', ' It has two sentences', '']
```

Stemming and lemmatization

Stemming and lemmatization are techniques used in natural language processing (NLP) to reduce words to their base form, known as the root word or stem. These techniques are used to standardize text and make it easier to analyze.

Stemming and lemmatization are similar in that they both involve reducing words to their base form, but they differ in how they achieve this. Stemming typically involves applying a set of rules to a word to remove suffixes and other word endings, while lemmatization involves using a vocabulary and morphological analysis to determine the lemma, or base form, of a word.

Here's an example of how to perform stemming and lemmatization in Python using the Natural Language Toolkit (NLTK) library:

```python
import nltk

# Perform stemming using the Porter stemmer
stemmer = nltk.PorterStemmer()
print(stemmer.stem("running"))  # Output: "run"
print(stemmer.stem("jumps"))  # Output: "jump"

# Perform lemmatization using the WordNet lemmatizer
lemmatizer = nltk.WordNetLemmatizer()
print(lemmatizer.lemmatize("running"))  # Output: "running"
print(lemmatizer.lemmatize("jumps"))  # Output: "jump"
```

The output of this code shows that the Porter stemmer reduces the words "running" and "jumps" to "run" and "jump," respectively, while the WordNet lemmatizer reduces them to "running" and "jump."

Stemming and lemmatization are useful for tasks such as text classification and information retrieval, where it is important to compare the meanings of words rather than their specific forms. For example, a search engine might use stemming or lemmatization to return results for a search query regardless of whether the search term is singular or plural.

However, it is important to note that stemming and lemmatization can sometimes produce results that are not actual words, and they can also lose important information about the context and meaning of a word. For example, the stem of the word "jumps" is "jump", but this stem is not an actual word and does not convey the same meaning as the original word. In contrast, lemmatization produces a word that is a valid English word, but it may not always be the most appropriate form for the specific context in which the word is used.

Stemming and lemmatization are useful techniques for reducing words to their base form in NLP tasks. They can be useful for standardizing text and comparing the meanings of words, but it is important to consider the potential trade-offs and limitations of these techniques when using them in real-world applications.

Stop word removal

Stop words are common words that are typically filtered out during natural language processing (NLP) tasks because they do not provide much meaningful information. Examples of stop words include words such as "a", "an", "the", and "of."

Stop words can be removed from a piece of text in order to reduce the size of the data and focus on the more important words. This can be useful for tasks such as text classification and information retrieval, where the frequency and order of the remaining words can be more indicative of the meaning and context of the text.

In Python, stop words can be removed using various libraries and techniques. One option is to use the Natural Language Toolkit (NLTK) library, which provides a list of English stop words that can be used as a reference. Here's an example of how to remove stop words from a piece of text using NLTK:

```python
import nltk
from nltk.corpus import stopwords

# Get the list of English stop words
stop_words = set(stopwords.words("english"))

# Tokenize the text and remove stop words
text = "This is a piece of text that we want to process."
tokens = nltk.word_tokenize(text)
filtered_tokens = [token for token in tokens if token not in stop_words]
print(filtered_tokens)
```

The output of this code would be:

```
['This', 'piece', 'text', 'want', 'process', '.']
```

Another option is to use the **gensim** library, which provides a function called **simple_preprocess**() that can be used to tokenize a piece of text and remove stop words.

Here's an example of how to use this function:

```
from gensim.parsing.preprocessing import simple_preprocess

# Tokenize the text and remove stop words
text = "This is a piece of text that we want to process."
filtered_tokens = simple_preprocess(text)
print(filtered_tokens)
```

The output of this code would be:

```
['piece', 'text', 'want', 'process']
```

Both of these methods allow you to easily remove stop words from a piece of text, but there are some differences between them. The NLTK library provides a larger list of stop words and allows you to customize the list by adding or removing words, but it requires you to perform the tokenization step separately. On the other hand, the **simple_preprocess**() function in the **gensim** library combines tokenization and stop word removal in a single step, but it uses a smaller list of stop words that cannot be customized.

In addition to these libraries, there are other ways to remove stop words in Python. For example, you can use the **CountVectorizer** class from the **sklearn** library to create a bag-of-words model and specify the **stop_words** parameter to remove stop words.

Case conversion and punctuation removal

Case conversion and punctuation removal are common preprocessing techniques in natural language processing (NLP) that involve converting text to a uniform case and removing punctuation marks. These techniques are often used to standardize text and make it easier to process and analyze.

In Python, case conversion and punctuation removal can be performed using various methods and libraries. One option is to use the **lower**() and **upper**() methods to convert text to lowercase or uppercase, respectively. Here's an example of how to use these methods:

```
text = "This is a Piece of Text."

# Convert text to lowercase
lowercase_text = text.lower()
print(lowercase_text)  # Output: "this is a piece of text."

# Convert text to uppercase
uppercase_text = text.upper()
print(uppercase_text)  # Output: "THIS IS A PIECE OF TEXT."
```

To remove punctuation marks from a piece of text, you can use the **translate**() method in combination with the **string** library, which provides a list of ASCII punctuation characters that can be used as a reference. Here's an example of how to use these methods:

```
import string

text = "This is a piece of text!"

# Remove punctuation marks using the translate() method
translator = str.maketrans("", "", string.punctuation)
no_punctuation_text = text.translate(translator)
print(no_punctuation_text)  # Output: "This is a piece of text"
```

Another option is to use regular expressions to remove punctuation marks. Regular expressions are a powerful tool for matching and manipulating strings, and they can be used to specify complex patterns of characters to search for and replace. Here's an example of how to use regular expressions to remove punctuation marks:

```
import re

text = "This is a piece of text!"

# Remove punctuation marks using regular expressions
no_punctuation_text = re.sub(r'[^\w\s]', '', text)
print(no_punctuation_text)  # Output: "This is a piece of text"
```

Exploring Text Data: Tools and techniques for analysing text

Introduction

Text data is a rich and diverse source of information that can be used to gain insights and make informed decisions. In this section, we will explore various techniques and tools that can be used to analyze text data and extract meaningful insights from it. We will focus on descriptive statistics and visualizations and provide practical examples in Python to illustrate these techniques.

Descriptive statistics

Descriptive statistics are statistical techniques used to summarize and describe the characteristics of a dataset. They can be used to understand the distribution, central tendency, and dispersion of data. In the context of text data, we can use descriptive statistics to get a sense of the overall structure and content of the data. For example, we can calculate the word count, vocabulary size, and frequency of each word in the text.

In Python, we can use the **Counter** class from the **collections** module to easily calculate the word frequency in a list of documents:

```
from collections import Counter

# Create a list of documents
documents = [
    "The cat sat on the mat.",
    "The cat was tired after playing with the mouse.",
    "The mouse ran away from the cat.",
    "The cat chased the mouse down the street."
]

# Tokenize the documents (i.e., split them into individual words)
tokens = [word for doc in documents for word in doc.split()]

# Calculate the word frequency
word_counts = Counter(tokens)
print(word_counts)
```

This will output a dictionary of word counts, where the keys are the words and the values are the number of times they appear in the text:

```
Counter({'The': 4, 'cat': 4, 'the': 2, 'on': 1, 'mat.': 1, 'was': 1, 'tired': 1, 'after': 1, 'playing': 1, 'with': 1, 'mouse.': 1, 'ran': 1, 'away': 1, 'from': 1, 'chased': 1, 'down': 1, 'street.': 1})
```

We can also use the **len** function to calculate the vocabulary size (i.e., the number of unique words in the text):

```
vocab_size = len(word_counts)
print(vocab_size)
```

This will output the vocabulary size:

```
16
```

Visualizations

Visualizations can be an effective way to explore and understand text data. They can help us identify patterns, trends, and relationships in the data that may not be immediately apparent from the raw data. There are many different types of visualizations that can be used to analyze text data, including word clouds, bar plots, and scatter plots.

Word clouds

A word cloud is a visual representation of the frequency of words in a text. It is a useful tool for quickly getting a sense of the most common words in a text and the overall tone of the text.

To create a word cloud in Python, we can use the **WordCloud** class from the **word cloud** library:

```python
from wordcloud import WordCloud
import matplotlib.pyplot as plt

# Create a list of words and their frequencies
words = ['cat', 'cat', 'cat', 'mouse', 'mouse']
freqs = [3, 3, 3, 2, 2]

# Create the word cloud
wordcloud = WordCloud().fit_words(dict(zip(words, freqs)))

# Display the word cloud
plt.imshow(wordcloud, interpolation='bilinear')
plt.axis("off")
plt.show()
```

This will create a word cloud with the words 'cat' and 'mouse', where the size of the word reflects its frequency in the text.

Bar plots

Bar plots are used to compare the distribution of a categorical variable. They consist of a series of bars, with each bar representing a category and the height of the bar representing the frequency or percentage of observations in that category.

Here is an example of how to create a bar plot in Python using the **matplotlib** library:

```python
import matplotlib.pyplot as plt

# Define the categories and their frequencies
categories = ['cat', 'mouse']
freqs = [3, 2]

# Create the bar plot
plt.bar(categories, freqs)

# Show the plot
plt.show()
```

This will create a bar plot with two bars, one for the 'cat' category and one for the 'mouse' category, where the height of the bars represents the frequency of each category.

Scatter plots

Scatter plots are a particularly useful type of visualization for text data analysis, as they allow you to see the relationship between two variables. For example, you might want to examine the relationship between the length of a document and the sentiment

of the text or between the frequency of certain words and the overall topic of the document.

To create a scatter plot in Python, you can use the matplotlib library. Here is an example of how you could create a scatter plot of the relationship between document length and sentiment using matplotlib:

```python
import matplotlib.pyplot as plt

# Create the scatter plot
plt.scatter(document_lengths, sentiments)

# Add labels to the axes
plt.xlabel('Document Length')
plt.ylabel('Sentiment')

# Show the plot
plt.show()
```

This code will create a scatter plot with the document lengths on the x-axis and the sentiments on the y-axis. The resulting plot will show the relationship between the two variables, and you can use it to identify any trends or patterns in the data.

Word frequencies and collocations

One of the most basic techniques for analyzing text data is to examine the frequencies of individual words within the text. This can help you to understand the overall content and theme of the text, as well as identify common patterns and trends. There are several ways to calculate word frequencies in Python, including using the Counter class from the collections module and the NLTK library.

Here is an example of how you could use the Counter class to calculate the word frequencies in a list of strings:

```python
from collections import Counter

# Calculate the word frequencies
word_frequencies = Counter(words)

# Print the most common words
print(word_frequencies.most_common(10))
```

This code will calculate the word frequencies for the list of strings stored in the word variable and then print the ten most common words. The output will be a list of tuples, with each tuple containing a word and its frequency.

Another useful technique for analyzing text data is to examine collocations, which are combinations of words that frequently occur together. Collocations can be a useful indicator of the themes and topics of a text and can help you to identify common patterns and trends in the data. To calculate collocations in Python, you can use the nltk library and the BigramAssocMeasures class.

Here is an example of how you could use the BigramAssocMeasures class to calculate the collocations in a list of strings: Here is an example of how you could use BigramAssocMeasures class to calculate the collocations in a list of strings:

```python
import nltk
from nltk.collocations import BigramAssocMeasures, BigramCollocationFinder

# Create the BigramCollocationFinder
finder = BigramCollocationFinder.from_words(words)

# Use the BigramAssocMeasures class to score the collocations
scorer = BigramAssocMeasures()
collocations = finder.score_ngrams(scorer.raw_freq)

# Print the top 10 collocations
print(collocations[:10])
```

This code will create a BigramCollocationFinder object from the list of strings stored in the **word** variable and then use the BigramAssocMeasures class to score the collocations based on their raw frequency. The resulting list of collocations will be sorted by score, with the most frequent collocations appearing first. The code will then print the top 10 collocations.

One of the benefits of using word frequencies and collocations to analyze text data is that they can provide a quick and easy way to understand the overall content and themes of a text. Additionally, these techniques can be useful for identifying common patterns and trends in the data, which can be useful for making predictions or making informed decisions based on the data.

However, there are also some limitations to using word frequencies and collocations for text data analysis. One limitation is that these techniques only provide a limited view of the text data, as they do not take into account the context or meaning of the words. Additionally, these techniques may not be the best choice for analyzing large datasets, as they can become cluttered and difficult to interpret when there is a large corpus.

Part-of-speech tagging

Part-of-speech (POS) tagging is a technique for labelling the words in a text with their corresponding parts of speech, such as nouns, verbs, adjectives, or adverbs. POS tagging can be a useful tool for analyzing text data, as it can help you to understand the structure and meaning of the text and can also be used to identify patterns and trends in the data. There are several libraries and tools available for POS tagging in Python, including the nltk library and the spaCy library.

Here is an example of how you could use the nltk library to perform POS tagging on a list of strings:

```python
import nltk

# Tokenize the text
tokens = nltk.word_tokenize(text)

# Perform POS tagging
pos_tags = nltk.pos_tag(tokens)

# Print the POS tags
print(pos_tags)
```

This code will tokenize the text stored in the **text** variable into a list of individual words and then perform POS tagging on the list of tokens. The resulting list of POS tags will be a list of tuples, with each tuple containing a word and its corresponding POS tag. The code will then print the list of POS tags.

Another option for POS tagging in Python is the spaCy library. Here is an example of how you could use the spaCy library to perform POS tagging on a list of strings:

```python
import spacy

# Load the English language model
nlp = spacy.load('en_core_web_sm')

# Tokenize the text
tokens = [token.text for token in nlp(text)]

# Perform POS tagging
pos_tags = [token.pos_ for token in nlp(text)]

# Print the POS tags
print(pos_tags)
```

This code will use the English language model from the spaCy library to tokenize the text stored in the **text** variable and then perform POS tagging on the list of tokens. The resulting list of POS tags will be a list of strings, with each string containing the POS tag for the corresponding token. The code will then print the list of POS tags.

One of the benefits of using POS tagging to analyze text data is that it can provide a detailed view of the structure and meaning of the text. POS tagging can be used to identify the main themes and topics of a text, as well as the relationships between words and phrases. Additionally, POS tagging can be useful for identifying patterns and trends in the data, which can be useful for making predictions or making informed decisions based on the data.

However, there are also some limitations to using POS tagging for text data analysis. One limitation is that POS tagging can be time-consuming and resource-intensive, particularly for large datasets. Additionally, POS tagging can be prone to errors, as it relies on the accuracy of the underlying language model. Finally, POS tagging does not take into account the context of the text, which can limit its usefulness for certain types of analysis.

Named entity recognition

Named entity recognition (NER) is a technique for extracting and identifying named entities in a text, such as people, organizations, locations, and events. NER can be a useful tool for analyzing text data, as it can help you to understand the content and context of the text and can also be used to identify patterns and trends in the data. There are several libraries and tools available for NER in Python, including the nltk library and the spaCy library.

Here is an example of how you could use the nltk library to perform NER on a list of strings:

```python
import nltk

# Tokenize the text
tokens = nltk.word_tokenize(text)

# Perform POS tagging
pos_tags = nltk.pos_tag(tokens)

# Use the nltk.ne_chunk function to perform NER
ner_tags = nltk.ne_chunk(pos_tags)

# Print the NER tags
print(ner_tags)
```

This code will tokenize the text stored in the **text** variable into a list of individual words and then perform POS tagging on the list of tokens. The **nltk.ne_chunk** function will then be used to perform NER on the list of POS tags, and the resulting NER tags will be a tree-like structure representing the named entities in the text. The code will then print the NER tags.

Another option for NER in Python is the spaCy library. Here is an example of how you could use the spaCy library to perform NER on a list of strings:

```python
import spacy

# Load the English language model
nlp = spacy.load('en_core_web_sm')

# Tokenize and perform NER on the text
doc = nlp(text)

# Print the NER tags
print([(token.text, token.ent_type_) for token in doc])
```

This code will use the English language model from the spaCy library to tokenize and perform NER on the text stored in the **text** variable. The resulting NER tags will be a list of tuples, with each tuple containing a word and its corresponding NER tag. The code will then print the NER tags.

One of the benefits of using NER to analyze text data is that it can provide a detailed view of the content and context of the text. NER can be used to identify the main actors and events in a text, as well as the relationships between them. Additionally, NER can be useful for identifying patterns and trends in the data, which can be useful for making predictions or making informed decisions based on the data.

However, there are also some limitations to using NER for text data analysis. One limitation is that NER can be time-consuming and resource-intensive, particularly for large datasets.

Representing Text Data: Techniques for converting text into numerical formats

CHAPTER
4

Introduction

When working with machine learning models, it is often necessary to convert text data into a numerical format. This is because many machine learning algorithms are designed to work with numerical data rather than text. There are several techniques that can be used to convert text data into numerical formats, and in this chapter, we will explore some of the most commonly used techniques.

Word embeddings

Word embedding is a technique in natural language processing (NLP) that represents words as numerical vectors in a high-dimensional space. There are different techniques for generating word embeddings, such as bag-of-words, term frequency-inverse document frequency (TF-IDF), and Word2vec. These techniques have different characteristics and are suitable for different tasks and applications.

One-hot encoding

One-hot encoding is a technique used to convert categorical variables, such as words or labels, into a numerical format. It works by creating a new binary column for each unique category in the data. For example, if we have a dataset with the categories "red," "yellow," and "blue," we would create three new binary columns, one for each category. The value in each column would be 1 if the original value was that category and 0 otherwise.

Here is an example of how one-hot encoding can be implemented in Python using the Pandas library:

```python
import pandas as pd

# Create a sample dataset with three categorical variables
data = {'color': ['red', 'yellow', 'blue', 'red', 'yellow'],
        'size': ['small', 'medium', 'large', 'small', 'medium'],
        'label': ['circle', 'triangle', 'circle', 'triangle', 'circle']}
df = pd.DataFrame(data)

# Use the Pandas get_dummies function to one-hot encode the categorical variables
df_encoded = pd.get_dummies(df, columns=['color', 'size', 'label'])

# The resulting dataframe will have six new columns, one for each unique category in the original data
print(df_encoded)
```

The output of this code will be a data frame with six new columns, one for each unique category in the original data. The values in these columns would be 1 if the original value was that category and 0 otherwise.

One-hot encoding is a simple and effective technique for converting categorical data into a numerical format. However, it can lead to a high-dimensional dataset with a large number of columns for each unique category. This can make the model more difficult to train and may require more computing resources.

Bag-of-words and n-grams

Bag-of-words is a technique used to represent text data in a numerical format. It works by creating a vocabulary of all the unique words in the text data and then creating a numerical representation of the text by counting the number of times each word appears in the text. This representation is called a bag-of-words because it is a collection of words, with the order of the words being discarded.

Here is an example of how bag-of-words can be implemented in Python using the Scikit-learn library:

```python
from sklearn.feature_extraction.text import CountVectorizer

# Create a list of documents
documents = ['This is the first document.',
            'This document is the second document.',
            'And this is the third one.',
            'Is this the first document?']

# Initialize the CountVectorizer
vectorizer = CountVectorizer()

# Use the fit_transform method to convert the documents into a numerical matrix
X = vectorizer.fit_transform(documents)

# The resulting matrix has one column for each unique word in the documents,
# and one row for each document
print(X)
```

The output of this code will be a sparse matrix with one column for each unique word in the documents and one row for each document. The values in the matrix represent the number of times each word appears in each document.

Bag-of-words is a simple and effective technique for converting text data into a numerical format. However, it does not take into account the order of the words in the text, which can be important in some applications. To address this, we can use a variation of bag-of-words called n-grams.

N-grams are sequences of n words in text data. For example, a 2-gram (also called a bigram) is a sequence of two words, a 3-gram (also called a trigram) is a sequence of three words, and so on. We can use n-grams to capture more contextual information in the text data by considering the sequence of words rather than just the individual words.

Here is an example of how n-grams can be implemented in Python using the Scikit-learn library:

```python
from sklearn.feature_extraction.text import CountVectorizer

# Create a list of documents
documents = ['This is the first document.',
            'This document is the second document.',
            'And this is the third one.',
            'Is this the first document?']

# Initialize the CountVectorizer with a range of n-grams from 1 to 3
vectorizer = CountVectorizer(ngram_range=(1, 3))

# Use the fit_transform method to convert the documents into a numerical matrix
X = vectorizer.fit_transform(documents)

# The resulting matrix has one column for each unique n-gram in the documents,
# and one row for each document
print(X)
```

The output of this code will be a numerical matrix with one row for each document and one column for each unique bigram in the documents. The values in the matrix represent the frequency of each bigram in the corresponding document.

Term frequency-inverse document frequency

TF-IDF is another technique that represents a piece of text as a fixed-length vector, but it takes into account the frequency of the words in the text relative to the frequency of the words in a larger corpus of text. The idea behind TF-IDF is that words that are more frequent in a document are more informative and should be given more weight, while words that are less frequent or common in the corpus should be given less weight.

In Python, TF-IDF can be implemented using the **TfidfVectorizer** class from the **sklearn** library, which works in a similar way to the **CountVectorizer** class. The **TfidfVectorizer** class requires you to specify the **input** parameter, which is a list of strings representing the text data, and the **max_features** parameter, which is the maximum number of features (i.e., words) to consider in the vocabulary.

Here's an example of how to use the **TfidfVectorizer** class to generate TF-IDF embeddings:

```python
from sklearn.feature_extraction.text import TfidfVectorizer

# Define the text data
text_data = ["cat say meow", "dog say bark"]

# Create the TfidfVectorizer object
vectorizer = TfidfVectorizer(input=text_data, max_features=1000)

# Generate the TF-IDF embeddings
embeddings = vectorizer.fit_transform(text_data)

# Print the TF-IDF embeddings
print(embeddings.toarray())
```

The output of this code will be a numerical matrix with one row for each document and one column for each unique word in the documents. The values in the matrix represent the TF-IDF weight of each word in the corresponding document.

TF-IDF is a useful technique for weighting the importance of words in a document based on their frequency and rarity. It can be used in conjunction with word embeddings to improve the performance of natural languages processing tasks, such as text classification and document similarity analysis.

Word2vec

One popular approach to training word embeddings is the word2vec algorithm. This algorithm was developed by Google and is based on a neural network architecture called a skip-gram model. The skip-gram model takes a word as input and tries to predict the surrounding words in the context. By training the model on a large dataset of text data, the word embeddings can be learned from the relationships between the words.

Here is an example of how the word2vec algorithm can be implemented in Python using the Gensim library:

```python
import gensim

# Load a dataset of text data
sentences = ['This is the first sentence.',
             'This is the second sentence.',
             'And this is the third sentence.']

# Train the word2vec model on the text data
model = gensim.models.Word2Vec(sentences, size=100, window=5, min_count=1, workers=4)

# Save the model to a file
model.save('word2vec.model')
```

The output of this code will be a trained word2vec model that has been saved to a file. The model can then be loaded to represent words as numerical vectors.

Here is an example of how the trained word2vec model can be used to represent words as numerical vectors:

```python
import gensim

# Load the trained word2vec model
model = gensim.models.Word2Vec.load('word2vec.model')

# Get the word embedding for a word
word = 'sentence'
vector = model.wv[word]

# The vector is a numerical representation of the word
print(vector)
```

The output of this code will be a numerical vector representing the word "sentence." The length of the vector will depend on the size parameter specified when training the model, which determines the dimensionality of the embedding space.

Overall, the word2vec algorithm is a popular and effective approach to training word embeddings. It is based on a neural network architecture that can learn the relationships between words from a large dataset of text data. The resulting word embeddings can be used as input to machine learning models and improve the performance of various natural language processing tasks.

Classification and Clustering: Organizing text data into categories

Introduction

Classification and clustering are two common techniques for organizing text data into categories. Classification involves assigning a label or category to each piece of data based on its characteristics. Clustering, on the other hand, involves grouping data into clusters based on similarities between the data points. Both classification and clustering can be useful for a wide range of applications, including text classification, document categorization, and topic modelling.

Introduction to classification and clustering

Classification is the process of assigning a label or category to a piece of data based on its characteristics. It is a supervised learning task, which means that it requires a labelled dataset to learn from. The goal of classification is to predict the correct label for new, unseen data.

There are many different algorithms and approaches that can be used for classification, including logistic regression, decision trees, and support vector machines (SVMs). These algorithms learn a model from the training data that can be used to predict the labels of new data.

For example, consider the task of classifying emails as spam or not spam. In this case, the label would be either "spam" or "not spam," and the characteristics of the data would be the words and phrases in the email. A classifier could be trained on a labelled dataset of emails, where each email is labelled as either "spam" or "not spam." The classifier would learn to predict the label for a new email based on the words and phrases in the email.

To train a classifier, we need to first convert the text data into a numerical format that can be used as input to the classifier. This can be done using techniques such as bag-of-words or word embeddings. Once the data is in a numerical format, we can then split it into a training set and a test set. The training set is used to fit the classifier model, while the test set is used to evaluate the performance of the model.

Clustering is the process of grouping data points into clusters based on similarities between the data points. It is an unsupervised learning task, which means that it does not require labelled data. Instead, the goal of clustering is to discover the underlying structure of the data and group similar data points together.

There are many different algorithms and approaches that can be used for clustering, including k-means clustering, hierarchical clustering, and density-based clustering. These algorithms work by iteratively partitioning the data into clusters based on some measure of similarity between the data points.

For example, consider the task of grouping a collection of documents into clusters based on their content. In this case, the characteristics of the data would be the words and phrases in the documents, and the goal would be to group together documents that are similar in content. A clustering algorithm could be used to identify the underlying structure of the data and group the documents into clusters based on their similarity.

To use a clustering algorithm, we first need to convert the text data into a numerical format that can be used as input to the algorithm. This can be done using techniques such as bag-of-words or word embeddings. Once the data is in a numerical format, we can apply the clustering algorithm to group the data into clusters.

Supervised and unsupervised learning

Both classification and clustering are examples of machine learning tasks, which means that they involve using algorithms to learn from data and make predictions or decisions. Machine learning can be divided into two main categories: supervised learning and unsupervised learning.

Supervised learning is a type of machine learning where the goal is to predict a label or output based on a set of input features. It requires a labelled dataset, which means that the output or label for each data point is already known. The goal of supervised learning is to learn a model that can predict the label for new, unseen data based on the input features. Examples of supervised learning tasks include classification and regression.

Unsupervised learning is a type of machine learning where the goal is to discover patterns or relationships in the data without any predetermined labels or outputs. It does not require a labelled dataset, and the goal is to learn from the data itself rather than from predefined labels. Examples of unsupervised learning tasks include clustering and dimensionality reduction.

Evaluation metrics for classification and clustering

Evaluation metrics are used to measure the performance of a classification or clustering model. Different metrics are appropriate for different types of tasks, and it is important to select the appropriate metric based on the characteristics of the data and the goals of the task.

For classification tasks, some common evaluation metrics include accuracy, precision, recall, and F1 score.

- Accuracy is the fraction of correct predictions made by the model out of all the predictions made. It is calculated as the number of correct predictions divided by the total number of predictions.
- Precision is the fraction of correct positive predictions made by the model out of all the positive predictions made. It is calculated as the number of true positive predictions divided by the total number of positive predictions made.
- The Recall is the fraction of correct positive predictions made by the model out of all the actual positive instances in the data. It is calculated as the number of true positive predictions divided by the total number of actual positive instances.
- The F1 score is a measure of the balance between precision and recall. It is calculated as the harmonic mean of precision and recall, with a higher score indicating a better balance.

For clustering tasks, some common evaluation metrics include adjusted R and index, adjusted mutual information, and silhouette score.

- Adjusted R and index is a measure of the similarity between the clusters produced by the model and the ground truth labels. It ranges from 1 (complete disagreement) to 1 (complete agreement), with a higher value indicating a better match.
- Adjusted mutual information is a measure of the mutual information between the clusters produced by the model and the ground truth labels.

It ranges from 0 (no mutual information) to 1 (complete mutual information), with a higher value indicating a better match.

- Silhouette score is a measure of the compactness and separation of the clusters. It ranges from -1 (poor separation) to 1 (good separation), with a higher value indicating better clustering.

Example classification and clustering algorithms

There are many different algorithms and approaches that can be used for the classification of textual data. Some common algorithms include:

- **Logistic regression**: Logistic regression is a linear classifier that uses a logistic function to predict the probability that a given input belongs to a particular class. It is often used for binary classification tasks but can also be used for multi-class classification.
- **Decision trees:** Decision trees are a type of tree-based classifier that uses a series of decision rules to predict the class label of a given input. Decision trees are easy to interpret and can handle both categorical and numerical data.
- **Support vector machines (SVMs):** SVMs are a type of linear classifier that uses a hyperplane to separate different classes. They are often used for classification tasks with high-dimensional data, such as text classification.

To use logistic regression for text classification, the text data must first be converted into a numerical format that can be used as input to the model. This can be done using techniques such as bag-of-words or word embeddings.

Here is an example of how logistic regression can be used for text classification in Python using the Scikit-learn library:

```
from sklearn.feature_extraction.text import CountVectorizer
from sklearn.linear_model import LogisticRegression

# Load the training data
X_train = ['This is the first document.',
           'This document is the second document.',
           'And this is the third one.',
           'Is this the first document?']
y_train = [0, 0, 1, 0]

# Convert the text data into numerical vectors using a CountVectorizer
vectorizer = CountVectorizer()
X_train = vectorizer.fit_transform(X_train)

# Initialize the classifier
clf = LogisticRegression()

# Fit the classifier to the training data
clf.fit(X_train, y_train)

# Test the classifier on some new data
X_test = ['This is a new document.', 'Is this the second document?']
X_test = vectorizer.transform(X_test)
predictions = clf.predict(X_test)
print(predictions)
```

The output of this code will be the predicted labels for the new data, which in this case will be [0, 0]. The labels are assigned based on the class with the highest probability, according to the logistic function learned by the model.

K-Means clustering

K-means clustering is a centroid-based algorithm that divides the data into a specified number of clusters. It works by iteratively assigning each data point to the closest cluster centroid and then updating the centroids to the mean of the data points in the cluster.

To use k-means clustering for text data, the text must first be converted into a numerical format that can be used as input to the algorithm. This can be done using techniques such as bag-of-words or word embeddings.

Here is an example of how k-means clustering can be used for text data in Python using the Scikit-learn library:

```python
from sklearn.cluster import KMeans

# Load the text data
X = ['This is the first document.',
    'This document is the second document.',
    'And this is the third one.',
    'Is this the first document?']

# Convert the text data into numerical vectors using a TfidfVectorizer
vectorizer = TfidfVectorizer()
X = vectorizer.fit_transform(X)

# Initialize the K-Means clusterer
kmeans = KMeans(n_clusters=2)

# Fit the clusterer to the data
kmeans.fit(X)

# Predict the cluster labels for new data
X_new = ['This is a new document.', 'Is this the second document?']
X_new = vectorizer.transform(X_new)
predictions = kmeans.predict(X_new)
print(predictions)
```

The output of this code will be the predicted cluster labels for the new data, which in this case will be [0, 1]. The cluster labels are assigned based on the closest cluster centroid to each data point.

Hierarchical clustering

Hierarchical clustering is an algorithm that builds a hierarchy of clusters, with each cluster being divided into smaller subclusters. There are two main types of hierarchical clustering: agglomerative and divisive. Agglomerative hierarchical clustering starts with each data point as a separate cluster and merges the closest clusters until all the data points are in a single cluster. Divisive hierarchical clustering starts with all the data points in a single cluster and divides the cluster into smaller subclusters until each data point is in its own cluster.

To use hierarchical clustering for text data, the text must first be converted into a numerical format that can be used as input to the algorithm. This can be done using techniques such as bag-of-words or word embeddings.

Here is an example of how hierarchical clustering can be used for text data in Python using the Scikit-learn library:

```python
from sklearn.feature_extraction.text import TfidfVectorizer
from sklearn.cluster import AgglomerativeClustering

# Load the text data
X = ['This is the first document.',
     'This document is the second document.',
     'And this is the third one.',
     'Is this the first document?']

# Convert the text data into numerical vectors using a TfidfVectorizer
vectorizer = TfidfVectorizer()
X = vectorizer.fit_transform(X)

# Initialize the Agglomerative Clustering model
model = AgglomerativeClustering(n_clusters=2)

# Fit the model to the data
model.fit(X)

# Predict the cluster labels for new data
X_new = ['This is a new document.', 'Is this the second document?']
X_new = vectorizer.transform(X_new)
predictions = model.fit_predict(X_new)
print(predictions)
```

The output of this code will be the predicted cluster labels for the new data, which in this case will be [0, 1]. The cluster labels are assigned based on the hierarchy of clusters built by the model.

Hierarchical clustering can be useful for tasks such as document categorization and topic modelling, where the goal is to discover the underlying structure of the data. It can also be used for information retrieval, where the goal is to group similar documents together for a more efficient search.

Sequence Analysis: Working with sequential data in NLP

CHAPTER 6

Introduction

In natural language processing (NLP), sequential data refers to data that is organized in temporal or sequential order. This can include data such as text, audio, and video, where the order of the data points is important in understanding the overall content or meaning.

One common example of sequential data in NLP is text data, where the order of the words in a sentence or paragraph conveys the meaning of the text. For example, in the sentence "The cat sat on the mat," the word "cat" refers to a specific animal, and the word "sat" indicates that the cat is in a state of rest. If the words were rearranged to say "The sat cat on the mat," the meaning of the sentence would be completely different.

Another example of sequential data in NLP is audio data, such as speech recordings. In this case, the order of the words and sounds is important in understanding the spoken message. For example, if someone says, "I'm going to the store," the meaning of the sentence is clear. However, if the words are rearranged to say "To the store going I'm," the meaning becomes unclear.

In addition to text and audio data, video data can also be considered sequential data in NLP. In a video, the order of the frames and their corresponding audio is important in understanding the content of the video.

Working with sequential data in NLP

There are many approaches to working with sequential data in NLP, and the specific approach will depend on the specific task at hand. Here are a few common approaches:

- **Tokenization**: Tokenization is the process of breaking down a piece of text into smaller units, such as individual words or subwords. This is a common preprocessing step in NLP and can be done using various techniques, such as splitting into spaces or using regular expressions.
- **N-grams**: An n-gram is a contiguous sequence of n items from a given sample of text or speech. N-grams are commonly used in NLP as a way to capture the context and meaning of a word or phrase. For example, a bigram (2-gram) of the sentence "The cat sat on the mat" would be "The cat," "the cat sat," "sat on," "on the," and "the mat."
- **Sequence labelling**: Sequence labelling is a task in NLP where the goal is to assign a label to each element in a sequence. This can be used for tasks such as named entity recognition, where the goal is to identify and label named entities (such as people, organizations, and locations) in a piece of text.
- **Sequence-to-sequence models**: Sequence-to-sequence models are a type of neural network architecture commonly used for tasks such as machine translation, where the input is a sequence in one language and the output is a corresponding sequence in another language. These models typically use encoder-decoder architecture, where the input sequence is first passed through an encoder to generate a fixed-length representation, and then this representation is passed through a decoder to generate the output sequence.
- **Recurrent neural networks (RNNs)**: RNNs are a type of neural network that is specifically designed to handle sequential data. They do this by introducing a hidden state that is passed from one-time step to the next, allowing the network to maintain information about the previous time steps as it processes the current input. RNNs are commonly used in NLP tasks such as language modelling and text generation.

Sequence tagging

Sequence tagging is a common task in natural language processing (NLP), where the goal is to assign a tag or label to each element in a sequence. This can be used for tasks such as named entity recognition, part-of-speech tagging, and chunking, where the goal is to identify and label specific types of words or phrases in a piece of text.

One common approach to sequence tagging is to use supervised learning, where the model is trained on a labelled dataset and then makes predictions on new, unseen data. The model is typically trained to maximize the accuracy of its predictions by minimizing the error between the predicted labels and the true labels in the training data.

Named entity recognition

Named entity recognition (NER) is the task of identifying and labelling named entities (such as people, organizations, and locations) in a piece of text. This can be useful for tasks such as information extraction, where the goal is to extract specific pieces of information from a large dataset.

For example, a company may have a large dataset of customer reviews and want to extract specific information such as the product being reviewed, the company being reviewed, and the location of the customer. NER can be used to automatically label these named entities in the text, making it easier to extract the desired information.

Here's an example of how to perform NER in Python using spaCy:

```python
import spacy

# Load the English language model
nlp = spacy.load('en_core_web_sm")

# Define a sentence to process
sentence = "Apple is based in Cupertino, California and was founded by Steve Jobs and Steve Wozniak."

# Process the sentence with the model
doc = nlp(sentence)

# Iterate over the entities in the document and print their labels
for ent in doc.ents:
    print(ent.text, ent.label_)
```

This code will output the following labels for the named entities in the sentence:

```
Apple ORG
Cupertino GPE
California GPE
Steve Jobs PERSON
Steve Wozniak PERSON
```

Part-of-speech tagging

Part-of-speech tagging is the task of labelling the words in a sentence with their corresponding part of speech (such as nouns, verbs, adjectives, etc.). This can be useful for tasks such as text classification, where the goal is to classify a piece of text into a specific category based on its content.

For example, a company may have a large dataset of customer reviews and want to classify the reviews as positive or negative. Part-of-speech tagging can be used to identify specific words or phrases that are indicative of a positive or negative sentiment, allowing the model to make more accurate classification decisions.

Here's an example of how to perform part-of-speech tagging in Python using spaCy:

```python
import spacy

# Load the English language model
nlp = spacy.load("en_core_web_sm")

# Define a sentence to process
sentence = "The cat sat on the mat."

# Process the sentence with the model
doc = nlp(sentence)

# Iterate over the tokens in the document and print their part-of-speech tags
for token in doc:
    print(token.text, token.pos_)
```

This code will output the following part-of-speech tags for the words in the sentence:

```
The DET
cat NOUN
sat VERB
on ADP
the DET
mat NOUN
. PUNCT
```

Chunking

Chunking is the task of extracting phrases from a sentence that represent a specific unit of meaning (such as noun phrases or verb phrases). This can be useful for tasks such as text summarization, where the goal is to generate a summary of a longer piece of text.

For example, a news organization may have a large dataset of articles and want to generate a summary of each article to include in a news feed. Chunking can be used to identify the most important phrases in the article, allowing the model to generate a concise summary that captures the main points of the article.

Here's an example of how to perform chunking in Python using spaCy:

```python
import spacy

# Load the English language model
nlp = spacy.load("en_core_web_sm")

# Define a sentence to process
sentence = "The cat sat on the mat."

# Process the sentence with the model
doc = nlp(sentence)

# Iterate over the chunks in the document and print their text
for chunk in doc.noun_chunks:
    print(chunk.text)
```

This code will output the following noun phrases for the sentence:

```
The cat
the mat
```

Text Generation: Creating text using machine learning techniques

Introduction to text generation

Text generation is a subfield of natural language processing (NLP) that focuses on using machine learning techniques to generate text similar to human-written text. It has a wide range of applications, including language translation, content creation, and language modelling.

One practical example of text generation is using a machine learning model to translate text from one language to another. For example, a machine learning model could be trained on a large dataset of translated sentences in order to accurately translate new sentences from one language to another.

Another practical example is using text generation to create new content, such as articles or social media posts. This can be useful for businesses that need to generate a large volume of content quickly or for individuals who want to create unique content but may not have the time or writing skills to do so manually.

Text generation can also be used for language modelling, which involves predicting the next word in a sentence or paragraph given a sequence of previous words. This can be used to improve the accuracy of natural languages processing tasks, such as speech recognition and language translation.

In summary, text generation is a powerful tool for creating human-like text using machine-learning techniques and has a wide range of practical applications in fields such as language translation, content creation, and language modelling.

Language models and sequence-to-sequence models

There are two main types of machine learning models that are commonly used for text generation: language models and sequence-to-sequence models.

Language models: Language models are trained to predict the likelihood of a given sequence of words. They are used to generate text by sampling the predicted probability distribution of words at each time step. Language models can be trained on a variety of text datasets, including books, articles, and social media posts.

One practical example of using a language model for text generation is generating product descriptions for an e-commerce website. A language model could be trained on a large dataset of product descriptions and then used to generate new descriptions for products added to the website. This can save time and resources for the e-commerce company, as they would not have to manually write descriptions for each new product.

Another practical example is using a language model to generate personalized emails or social media posts. A language model could be trained on a dataset of emails or social media posts and then used to generate new messages tailored to the recipient. For example, a language model could be used to generate personalized email marketing campaigns or to generate personalized social media posts for a business's followers.

Sequence-to-sequence models: Sequence-to-sequence models, on the other hand, are trained to map a sequence of input words to a sequence of output words. They are commonly used for tasks such as language translation and summarization.

One practical example of using a sequence-to-sequence model for text generation is a machine translation. A sequence-to-sequence model could be trained on a large dataset of translated sentences and then used to translate new sentences from one language to another. This can be useful for businesses that operate in multiple languages, as it can save time and resources that would be spent on manually translating text.

Another practical example is using a sequence-to-sequence model for text summarization. A model could be trained on a dataset of long articles and then used to generate shorter summaries of the articles. This can be useful for news websites or other organizations that need to quickly produce summaries of large amounts of text.

In summary, language models and sequence-to-sequence models are two types of machine learning models that can be used for text generation. They are commonly used for tasks such as language translation, summarization, and generating human-like text based on a prompt. Text generation has a wide range of practical applications, including creating personalized emails and social media posts, generating product descriptions for e-commerce websites, and translating text from one language to another.

Text generation applications and challenges

Text generation has a wide range of applications, including language translation, content creation, and language modelling. Some practical examples of text generation applications include:

- **Language translation**: Machine learning models can be trained on large datasets of translated sentences and then used to translate new sentences from one language to another. This can be useful for businesses that operate in multiple languages or for individuals who need to translate text for personal or professional purposes.
- **Content creation**: Text generation can be used to create new content, such as articles or social media posts. This can be useful for businesses that need to generate a large volume of content quickly or for individuals who want to create unique content but may not have the time or writing skills to do so manually.
- **Language modelling:** Text generation can be used for language modelling, which involves predicting the next word in a sentence or paragraph given a sequence of previous words. This can be used to improve the accuracy of natural languages processing tasks, such as speech recognition and language translation.

While text generation has many practical applications, it also comes with its own set of challenges. Some of the challenges of text generation include the following:

- Ensuring the generated text is accurate and grammatically correct: One challenge of text generation is ensuring that the generated text is accurate and free of errors. This can be difficult, as machine learning models may generate text that is nonsensical or contains grammatical errors.
- Ensuring the generated text is coherent and makes sense: Another challenge of text generation is ensuring that the generated text is coherent and makes sense. Machine learning models may generate text that is disjointed or unrelated to the prompt, which can be confusing or difficult to understand.
- Ensuring the generated text is diverse and not biased: Text generation models can sometimes generate text that is biased or repetitive, as they are trained on a specific dataset. Ensuring that the generated text is diverse and not biased is an important challenge of text generation.

In summary, text generation has a wide range of practical applications, including language translation, content creation, and language modelling. However, it also comes with its own set of challenges, such as ensuring the generated text is accurate, coherent, and diverse.

Implementation of text generation

There are several libraries and frameworks in Python that can be used for text generation using machine learning techniques. In this chapter, we will explore the implementation of text generation using a popular library: TensorFlow.

TensorFlow is a machine learning library developed by Google. It has a wide range of applications, including text generation. To use TensorFlow for text generation, you will need to install the library and import it into your Python code. Here is an example of how to install and import TensorFlow in Python:

```
pip install tensorflow

import tensorflow as tf
```

Once TensorFlow is installed and imported, you can use it to build and train a machine-learning model for text generation. There are several types of models that can be used for text generation, including language models and sequence-to-sequence models.

To build a language model using TensorFlow, you will need to define the model architecture and choose an optimization algorithm and loss function. You can then use the fit() function to train the model on a dataset of text. Here is an example of how to build and train a simple language model using TensorFlow:

```
model = tf.keras.Sequential()
model.add(tf.keras.layers.Embedding(input_dim=vocab_size, output_dim=embedding_dim))
model.add(tf.keras.layers.LSTM(units=hidden_dim))
model.add(tf.keras.layers.Dense(units=vocab_size, activation='softmax'))


model.compile(optimizer='adam', loss='categorical_crossentropy')


model.fit(X_train, y_train, epochs=5, batch_size=128)
```

Once the model is trained, you can use it to generate text by providing a prompt and sampling from the predicted probability distribution of words at each time step. Here is an example of how to use the trained model to generate text:

```python
def generate_text(model, prompt, temperature=1.0):
    tokens = tokenize(prompt)
    while True:
        encoded_prompt = encode(tokens, vocab_size)
        encoded_prompt = tf.expand_dims(encoded_prompt, 0)
        predictions = model.predict(encoded_prompt, steps=1)[0]
        next_token = sample(predictions, temperature)
        tokens.append(next_token)
        if next_token == '<END>':
            break
    return decode(tokens, vocab_size)


generated_text = generate_text(model, "The quick brown fox jumps over the lazy dog.")
print(generated_text)
```

Language Translation: Translating the text from one language to another

Introduction to machine translation

Machine translation, also known as automated or automatic translation, is the process of using learning algorithms to translate text or speech from one language to another. This technology has come a long way in recent years, with many machine translation systems now able to produce translations that are almost as good as those produced by human translators.

One of the main benefits of machine translation is that it can save time and effort compared to manually translating text. For example, consider a business that needs to translate a contract from English to Spanish. With machine translation, the entire process can be automated, allowing the business to get the translation done quickly and efficiently.

Another benefit of machine translation is that it can be used in a variety of different contexts. For example, it can be used to translate websites and other online content, making it easier for people to access information in their own language. It can also be used to translate documents, such as contracts and legal documents, as well as emails and other written communications.

Practical examples of machine translation

- **Business:** One common use of machine translation is for businesses that want to expand their reach to a global market. Imagine a company based in the United States that wants to sell its products in Spain. The company can use machine translation to translate its website, product descriptions, and other marketing materials into Spanish. This way, potential customers in Spain can easily understand the company's offerings and make informed purchasing decisions.

- **Government organizations:** Government organizations also use machine translation to communicate with citizens and stakeholders who speak different languages. For example, a city government may use machine translation to translate public announcements and documents into multiple languages so that all residents can access important information
- **Educational institutions:** Educational institutions can also benefit from machine translation. For example, a university with a diverse student body may use machine translation to translate course materials and lectures into different languages. This can help students who speak languages other than English to better understand the material and succeed in their studies.
- **Online customer service:** Machine translation is also useful for online customer service. Imagine a customer in Germany who has a question about a product purchased from an online retailer based in the United States. The customer can use machine translation to communicate with the retailer in English, and the retailer can use machine translation to respond in German. This allows the customer to get the help they need without having to speak English fluently.

Machine translation is a powerful tool that can help businesses, organizations, and individuals communicate with people who speak different languages. With the right software and strategies, machine translation can help facilitate cross-cultural communication and break down language barriers.

Translation models and techniques

Translation models and techniques are the methods and approaches that are used to translate text from one language to another. There are several different types of translation models and techniques, and each one has its own advantages and limitations. In this section, we will explore some of the most commonly used translation models and techniques, along with practical examples of how they are used in real-world situations.

- **Rule-based translation:** Rule-based translation, also known as direct translation, is a method of translation that relies on a set of pre-defined rules and dictionaries to translate text from one language to another. This approach is based on the idea that language can be broken down into a set of discrete rules that can be applied to translate text from one language to another.

One practical example of rule-based translation is the use of translation software such as Google Translate. When a user inputs a piece of text into the software, the software looks up the words in its dictionary and applies a set of rules to translate the text into the desired language.

- **Statistical machine translation:** Statistical machine translation is a method of translation that uses statistical models to translate text from one language to another. This approach relies on large amounts of parallel text, which is the text that has been translated from one language to another by a human translator. The statistical model uses this parallel text to learn the patterns and correlations between the source language and the target language, and it uses this information to translate new text.

  One practical example of statistical machine translation is the use of translation software such as DeepL. This software uses a statistical machine translation model that has been trained on a large dataset of parallel text to translate text from one language to another.

- **Neural machine translation**: Neural machine translation is a method of translation that uses artificial neural networks to translate text from one language to another. This approach relies on deep learning techniques to understand the relationships between words and phrases in the source language and the target language.

  One practical example of neural machine translation is the use of translation software such as Systran. This software uses a neural machine translation model that has been trained on a large dataset of parallel text to translate text from one language to another.

- **Hybrid machine translation:** Hybrid machine translation is a method of translation that combines the strengths of different translation models and techniques to achieve the best possible translation results. This approach may use a combination of rule-based, statistical, and neural machine translation techniques to translate text from one language to another.

  One practical example of hybrid machine translation is the use of translation software such as Microsoft Translator. This software uses a hybrid machine translation model that combines the strengths of different translation models and techniques to achieve the best possible translation results.

Evaluation metrics for translation

Evaluation metrics are used to measure the quality of a translation and determine how well it meets the desired criteria. These metrics are important for businesses, organizations, and individuals who rely on translations to communicate with people who speak different languages, as they help to ensure that the translations are accurate and effective. In this section, we will explore some of the most commonly used evaluation metrics for translation, along with practical examples of how they are used in real-world situations.

- **BLEU Score**

  The BLEU (Bilingual Evaluation Understudy) score is a metric that measures the quality of a machine-translated text by comparing it to a reference translation that has been produced by a human translator. The BLEU score is calculated by comparing the n-grams (sequences of words) in the machine-translated text to the n-grams in the reference translation, and it is expressed as a percentage. A higher BLEU score indicates a higher level of accuracy in the machine-translated text.

  One practical example of the use of the BLEU score is in the evaluation of machine translation software. When a company is considering purchasing machine translation software, it can use the BLEU score to compare the accuracy of the translations produced by different software options.

- **Word error rate**

  The word error rate (WER) is a metric that measures the number of errors in a machine-translated text by comparing it to a reference translation that has been produced by a human translator. The WER is calculated by dividing the total number of errors in the machine-translated text by the total number of words in the reference translation, and it is expressed as a percentage. A lower WER indicates a higher level of accuracy in the machine-translated text.

  One practical example of the use of the WER is in the evaluation of speech-to-text translation software. When a company is considering purchasing a speech-to-text translation software, it can use the WER to compare the accuracy of the translations produced by different software options.

- **TER Score**

  The TER (Translation Error Rate) score is a metric that measures the quality of a machine-translated text by comparing it to a reference translation that has been produced by a human translator. The TER score is calculated by comparing the machine-translated text to the reference translation at the word and phrase level, and it is expressed as a percentage. A lower TER score indicates a higher level of accuracy in the machine-translated text.

One practical example of the use of the TER score is in the evaluation of translation memories. Translation memories are databases that store translated text and can be used to speed up the translation process by suggesting previously translated phrases or sentences. When a company is considering purchasing translation memory software, it can use the TER score to compare the accuracy of the translations produced by different software options.

- **Human evaluation**
  Human evaluation is a method of evaluating the quality of a translation by having it reviewed by a human translator. This approach involves having a human translator compare the machine-translated text to the reference translation and rate the overall quality of the translation on a scale such as "excellent," "good," "fair," or "poor."

  One practical example of the use of human evaluation metrics in language translation might involve a company that is looking to translate its marketing materials into multiple languages. The company could have a team of translators, and bilingual speakers review the translations and provide feedback on their accuracy, fluency, adequacy, style, and cultural appropriateness. This feedback could then be used to identify areas where the translations could be improved and make any necessary adjustments to ensure that the marketing materials are effective in all target languages.

Implementation of language translation

One common method for implementing language translation in Python is through the use of machine translation APIs. These APIs are provided by companies such as Google, Microsoft, and IBM, and they allow users to access the company's machine translation technology through a simple API call.

To use a machine translation API in Python, you will need to first sign up for an API key from the provider. Once you have an API key, you can use it to make requests to the API and receive a translated text in return.

Here is an example of how you might use the Google Translate API in Python to translate a string of text from English to Spanish:

```
import requests

def translate(text, target_language):
  api_key = "YOUR_API_KEY"
  base_url = "https://translation.googleapis.com/language/translate/v2"
  params = {
    "q": text,
    "target": target_language,
    "key": api_key
  }
  response = requests.get(base_url, params=params)
  translation = response.json()["data"]["translations"][0]["translatedText"]
  return translation

text = "Hello, world!"
translated_text = translate(text, "es")
print(translated_text)
```

This code uses the **requests** library to send a request to the Google Translate API with the text to be translated and the target language. The API returns a JSON response, which is then parsed to extract the translated text. The translated text is then printed to the console.

Another way to implement language translation in Python is through the use of machine learning models. There are several open-source machine learning libraries available for Python, such as TensorFlow and PyTorch, that can be used to train machine learning models for language translation.

To train a machine learning model for language translation, you will need a large dataset of the translated text. You can use this dataset to train a machine learning model to predict the translation of a given piece of text based on the patterns it has learned from the training data. The PyTorch implementation is not covered in this book.

Information Extraction: Extracting structured data from unstructured text

## CHAPTER 9

Introduction to information extraction

Information extraction (IE) is the process of extracting structured information from unstructured text data. This structured information can include things like entities, relationships, and events mentioned in the text.

IE is an important task in natural language processing (NLP) because it allows us to extract useful information from large amounts of unstructured text data and use it for various purposes, such as information retrieval, summarization, and question-answering.

Information extraction is used to extract structured data from unstructured text sources. It involves identifying specific pieces of information, such as names, dates, and locations, and organizing them into a structured format. This can be done manually or through the use of specialized software or tools.

One common use case for information extraction is in the field of information retrieval. When we search for something on the internet, we often use a search engine to find relevant results. However, the results we get are often a mix of structured and unstructured data. Information extraction can be used to extract structured data from these results, making it easier for the search engine to understand and rank them.

Information extraction can be used in a wide variety of applications, including:

- **News monitoring**: Organizations can use information extraction to automatically extract news articles relevant to their industry or specific topics of interest. For example, a financial company might use information extraction to track mentions of its stock price or competitors in the news.

- **Social media analysis:** Information extraction can be used to extract data from social media posts, such as hashtags, mentions of specific users or products, and sentiment. This can be used to track the reach and impact of social media campaigns or to identify trends or issues related to a particular product or service.
- **Customer service:** Information extraction can be used to automatically extract data from customer service inquiries, such as the customer's name, account number, and issue. This can help companies more efficiently route and respond

Practical examples of information extraction include:

- **Entity extraction:** This involves identifying and extracting entities such as people, organizations, and locations from the text. For example, if you have a news article about the launch of a new product by Microsoft, you can use entity extraction to identify the company "Microsoft", and the product is launched.
- **Relationship extraction:** This involves identifying and extracting relationships between entities in the text. For example, if you have a news article about a merger between two companies, you can use relationship extraction to identify the companies involved in the merger and the nature of the relationship (e.g., merger, acquisition, etc.).
- **Event extraction:** This involves identifying and extracting events mentioned in the text. For example, if you have a news article about a political rally, you can use event extraction to identify the event (e.g., political rally), the location, and the participants.

Relation extraction

Relation extraction is a subfield of information extraction that involves identifying and extracting relationships between entities in text. These relationships can be between people, organizations, locations, and other types of entities.

Examples of relation extraction include:

- **Identifying relationships between people:** This can be useful for tasks such as author disambiguation, where you want to identify the relationship between different authors with the same name. For example, you can use relation extraction to identify that "John Smith" and "John Smith Jr." are father and son.

- **Identifying relationships between organizations:** This can be useful for tasks such as market analysis, where you want to identify relationships between different companies. For example, you can use relation extraction to identify that "Microsoft" acquired "LinkedIn."
- **Identifying relationships between locations:** This can be useful for tasks such as event tracking, where you want to identify relationships between locations and events. For example, you can use relation extraction to identify that an event took place in "New York City."

There are several approaches to relation extraction, including rule-based, dictionary-based, and machine learning-based approaches.

In a rule-based approach, you define a set of rules to identify and extract relationships from the text. For example, you can define a rule that says if a sentence contains the words "Microsoft" and "acquired," then there is a relationship between "Microsoft" and the entity mentioned after "acquired." While this approach can be effective for simple cases, it becomes impractical as the complexity of the text increases.

In a dictionary-based approach, you use a predefined list of relationships to extract information from the text. For example, you can use a list of company acquisitions to identify relationships between companies. While this approach can be effective for simple cases, it becomes impractical as the complexity of the text increases, and it may not be able to handle novel relationships.

In a machine learning-based approach, you use a machine learning model to extract relationships from the text. This approach is more flexible and can handle a wider range of text complexity, but it requires a large amount of annotated data to train the model.

There are several tools and libraries available for relation extraction in Python, including Stanford CoreNLP, spaCy, and OpenIE. These tools provide various features, such as entity recognition, dependency parsing, and relation extraction, which can be used to build relation extraction systems.

Here is an example of how you can use Stanford CoreNLP to extract relationships from the text in Python:

```
import os
from stanfordcorenlp import StanfordCoreNLP

# Set up the Stanford CoreNLP client
nlp = StanfordCoreNLP(os.environ["CORENLP_HOME"], lang="en")

# Annotate the text
text = "Microsoft acquired LinkedIn."
annotations = nlp.annotate(text, properties={
    "annotators": "tokenize,ssplit,pos,depparse",
    "outputFormat": "json"
})

# Extract the dependencies
deps = annotations["sentences"][0]["basicDependencies"]

# Iterate over the dependencies and extract the relationships
for dep in deps:
    if dep["dep"] == "nsubj":
        subject = dep["dependentGloss"]
    if dep["dep"] == "dobj":
        object = dep["dependentGloss"]
    if dep["dep"] == "root":
        verb = dep["dependentGloss"]

# Print the extracted relationship
print(f"{subject} {verb} {object}")

# Output: Microsoft acquired LinkedIn

# Clean up
nlp.close()
```

In this example, we use the Stanford CoreNLP API to annotate the text with dependency parse information. We then extract the dependencies and iterate over them to identify the subject, verb, and object of the sentence. Finally, we print the extracted relationship.

Event extraction

Event extraction is a subfield of information extraction that involves identifying and extracting events mentioned in the text. An event is a happening or occurrence that can be described and has some significance.

Examples of event extraction include:

- **Identifying events in news articles:** This can be useful for tasks such as news summarization, where you want to extract important events from a large number of articles. For example, you can use event extraction to identify that "Microsoft launched a new product."
- **Identifying events in social media posts:** This can be useful for tasks such as event tracking, where you want to identify events that are happening or have happened in a specific location. For example, you can use event extraction to identify that "There is a protest happening in New York City."
- **Identifying events in legal documents:** This can be useful for tasks such as contract analysis, where you want to extract important events and conditions mentioned in a contract. For example, you can use event extraction to identify that "Company A must pay Company B $100,000 upon the completion of the project."

There are several approaches to event extraction, including rule-based, dictionary-based, and machine learning-based approaches.

In a rule-based approach, you define a set of rules to identify and extract events from the text. For example, you can define a rule that says if a sentence contains the words "launched" and "product," then there is an event of a company launching a product. While this approach can be effective for simple cases, it becomes impractical as the complexity of the text increases.

In a dictionary-based approach, you use a predefined list of events to extract information from the text. For example, you can use a list of common business events (e.g., launch, acquisition, merger) to identify events in the text. While this approach can be effective for simple cases, it becomes impractical as the complexity of the text increases, and it may not be able to handle novel events.

In a machine learning-based approach, you use a machine learning model to extract events from the text. This approach is more flexible and can handle a wider range of text complexity, but it requires a large amount of annotated data to train the model.

There are several tools and libraries available for event extraction in Python, including Stanford CoreNLP, spaCy, and OpenIE. These tools provide various features, such as entity recognition, dependency parsing, and relation extraction, which can be used to build event extraction systems.

Here is an example of how you can use Stanford CoreNLP to extract events from the text in Python:

```
import os
from stanfordcorenlp import StanfordCoreNLP

# Set up the Stanford CoreNLP client
nlp = StanfordCoreNLP(os.environ["CORENLP_HOME"], lang="en")

# Annotate the text
text = "Microsoft launched a new product."
annotations = nlp.annotate(text, properties={
    "annotators": "tokenize,ssplit,pos,depparse",
    "outputFormat": "json"
})

# Extract the dependencies
deps = annotations["sentences"][0]["basicDependencies"]

# Iterate over the dependencies and extract the event
for dep in deps:
    if dep["dep"] == "nsubj":
        subject = dep["dependentGloss"]
    if dep["dep"] == "root":
        verb = dep["dependentGloss"]
    if dep["dep"] == "dobj":
        object = dep["dependentGloss"]

# Print the extracted event
print(f"{subject} {verb} {object}")

# Output: Microsoft launched a new product

# Clean up
nlp.close()
```

In this example, we use the Stanford CoreNLP API to annotate the text with dependency parse information. We then extract the dependencies and iterate over them to identify the subject, verb, and object of the sentence. Finally, we print the extracted event.

Named entity recognition

Named entity recognition (NER) is a subfield of information extraction that involves identifying and extracting named entities such as people, organizations, and locations from the text. Named entities are proper nouns that refer to specific individuals, organizations, or locations.

Examples of named entity recognition include:

- **Identifying people in news articles:** This can be useful for tasks such as author disambiguation, where you want to identify the people mentioned in an article. For example, you can use named entity recognition to identify that "Barack Obama" is a person.
- Identifying organizations in job postings: This can be useful for tasks such as job matching, where you want to identify the companies mentioned in a job posting. For example, you can use named entity recognition to identify that "Google" is an organization.
- Identifying locations in social media posts: This can be useful for tasks such as event tracking, where you want to identify the locations mentioned in social media posts. For example, you can use named entity recognition to identify that "New York City" is a location.

There are several approaches to named entity recognition, including rule-based, dictionary-based, and machine learning-based approaches.

In a rule-based approach, you define a set of rules to identify and extract named entities from the text. For example, you can define a rule that says if a word is capitalized and appears at the beginning of a sentence, it is a named entity. While this approach can be effective for simple cases, it becomes impractical as the complexity of the text increases.

In a dictionary-based approach, you use a predefined list of named entities to extract information from the text. For example, you can use a list of common names to identify people in the text. While this approach can be effective for simple cases, it becomes impractical as the complexity of the text increases, and it may not be able to handle novel named entities.

In a machine learning-based approach, you use a machine learning model to extract named entities from the text. This approach is more flexible and can handle a wider range of text complexity, but it requires a large amount of annotated data to train the model.

There are several tools and libraries available for named entity recognition in Python, including Stanford CoreNLP, spaCy, and OpenIE. These tools provide various features, such as entity recognition, dependency parsing, and relation extraction, which can be used to build named entity recognition systems.

Here is an example of how you can use Stanford CoreNLP to extract named entities from the text in Python:

```python
import os
from stanfordcorenlp import StanfordCoreNLP

# Set up the Stanford CoreNLP client
nlp = StanfordCoreNLP(os.environ["CORENLP_HOME"], lang="en")

# Annotate the text
text = "Barack Obama was the President of the United States."
annotations = nlp.annotate(text, properties={
    "annotators": "tokenize,ssplit,pos,ner",
    "outputFormat": "json"
})

# Extract the named entities
entities = annotations["sentences"][0]["entitymentions"]

# Iterate over the named entities and print their type and text
for entity in entities:
    print(f"{entity['ner']}: {entity['text']}")

# Output:
# PERSON: Barack Obama
# LOCATION: United States

# Clean up
nlp.close()
```

In this example, we use the Stanford CoreNLP API to annotate the text with named entity information. We then extract the named entities and iterate over them to print their type and text.

Text Summarization: Creating concise summaries of text data

Introduction to text summarization

Text summarization is the process of creating a concise and coherent summary of a large piece of text. This can be useful for a variety of applications, such as summarizing news articles, legal documents, or research papers.

Text summarization is a useful tool for a variety of applications, including information retrieval, content analysis, and document management. It can help users quickly and easily understand the main points of a large piece of text, saving them time and effort. It is also an important tool in the field of natural language processing, as it involves many of the same techniques and challenges as other natural language processing tasks, such as language translation and text classification.

There are two main types of text summarization: extractive and abstractive.

Extractive summarization involves selecting key phrases and sentences from the original text and piecing them together to create a summary. This type of summarization is often preferred because it is more accurate and reliable, as it relies on the actual content of the text. However, extractive summarization can sometimes result in a summary that is choppy and lacks coherence, as it may not capture the overall meaning and structure of the text.

Abstractive summarization, on the other hand, involves generating a summary that is not directly based on the original text. This type of summarization requires a more in-depth understanding of the text and often involves the use of natural language processing techniques to generate a summary that is more coherent and reads like a human-written summary. Abstractive summarization is more challenging to implement, but it has the potential to produce more accurate and engaging summaries.

There are a number of approaches to text summarization, including rule-based methods, statistical methods, and machine learning-based methods. Rule-based methods involve the use of pre-defined rules or heuristics to identify and select important information from the text. Statistical methods involve the use of mathematical models and algorithms to identify patterns and relationships in the text and generate a summary based on those patterns. Machine learning-based methods involve the use of machine learning algorithms to learn patterns and relationships in the text and generate a summary based on those patterns.

Extractive and abstractive summarization

Text summarization can be divided into two main categories: extractive and abstractive. Extractive summarization involves selecting key phrases and

sentences from the original text and piecing them together to create a summary. This type of summarization is often preferred because it is more accurate and reliable, as it relies on the actual content of the text. However, extractive summarization can sometimes result in a summary that is choppy and lacks coherence, as it may not capture the overall meaning and structure of the text.

Abstractive summarization, on the other hand, involves generating a summary that is not directly based on the original text. This type of summarization requires a more in-depth understanding of the text and often involves the use of natural language processing techniques to generate a summary that is more coherent and reads like a human-written summary. Abstractive summarization is more challenging to implement, but it has the potential to produce more accurate and engaging summaries.

In this section, we will take a closer look at both extractive and abstractive summarization, including practical examples of how to implement these techniques using Python. We will also discuss some of the challenges and considerations involved in text summarization and provide tips and best practices for achieving high-quality summaries.

Extractive summarization

Extractive summarization involves selecting key phrases and sentences from the original text to create a summary. This can be done manually by reading through the text and selecting the most important information or automatically using algorithms and natural language processing techniques to identify and extract key phrases and sentences.

One simple way to implement extractive summarization in Python is to use the Gensim library, which provides a number of tools and algorithms for text analysis and summarization. For example, the Gensim library includes a function called **summarize** that can be used to generate a summary of a given piece of text. Here is an example of how to use the **summarize** function in Python:

```python
from gensim.summarization import summarize

# original text
text = "This is a long piece of text that we want to summarize. It includes a variety of information and ideas, and we want to condense it into a shorter, more concise summary. Extractive summarization involves selecting key phrases and sentences from the original text, and piecing them together to create a summary. This can be done manually or automatically using algorithms and natural language processing techniques. Abstractive summarization, on the other hand, involves generating a summary that is not directly based on the original text, and requires a more in-depth understanding of the text. It often involves the use of natural language processing techniques to generate a summary that is more coherent and reads like a human-written summary."

# generate summary
summary = summarize(text)
print(summary)
```

This code will generate a summary of the original text using the **summarize** function from the Gensim library. The summary will be a shorter version of the original text, containing only the most important phrases and sentences.

Abstractive summarization

Abstractive summarization involves generating a summary that is not directly based on the original text. This type of summarization requires a more in-depth understanding of the text and often involves the use of natural language processing techniques to generate a summary that is more coherent and reads like a human-written summary. Abstractive summarization is more challenging to implement, but it has the potential to produce more accurate and engaging summaries.

There are a number of approaches to abstractive summarization, including the use of machine learning algorithms and deep learning techniques. One popular approach is to use encoder-decoder architectures, which consist of two separate neural networks: an encoder that processes the input text and a decoder that generates the summary.

To implement abstractive summarization in Python, you will need to use a machine learning library such as TensorFlow or PyTorch. Here is an example of how to implement abstractive summarization using Transformer:

```
import torch
import torch.nn as nn
import torch.optim as optim

# original text
text = "This is a long piece of text that we want to summarize. It includes a variety of information
and ideas, and we want to condense it into a shorter, more concise summary. Extractive summarization
involves selecting key phrases and sentences from the original text, and piecing them together to
create a summary. This can be done manually or automatically using algorithms and natural language
processing techniques. Abstractive summarization, on the other hand, involves generating a summary that
is not directly based on the original text, and requires a more in-depth understanding of the text. It
often involves the use of natural language processing techniques to generate a summary that is more
coherent and reads like a human-written summary."

# preprocessing
max_length = 100
vocab_size = 10000

# tokenize text
tokenizer = torch.hub.load('huggingface/pytorch-transformers', 'tokenizer', 'bert-base-cased')
text_sequences = tokenizer.encode(text, max_length=max_length)

# build model
model = torch.hub.load('huggingface/pytorch-transformers', 'model', 'bert-base-cased')
model.eval()

# generate summary
with torch.no_grad():
    input_tensor = torch.tensor([[text_sequences]])
    summary = model(input_tensor)[0]
    summary = torch.argmax(summary, dim=-1)
    summary = tokenizer.decode(summary.tolist()[0])
    print(summary)
```

This code will use the BERT transformer model from the hugging face/ Pytorch-transformers library to generate a summary of the original text. The summary will be generated by taking the maximum probability token at each time step and decoding the resulting sequence using the BERT tokenizer. This will produce a summary that is not directly based on the original text but is generated by the transformer model based on its understanding of the text.

Evaluation metrics for summarization

Evaluating the quality of a text summarization is a complex task, as it often involves comparing the summary to the original text and assessing how well the summary captures the key points and ideas of the original text. There are a number of different evaluation metrics that can be used to assess the quality of a summary, including:

- ROUGE (Recall-Oriented Understudy for Gisting Evaluation) measures the overlap between the summary and the original text in terms of n-grams, where n can be 1 (unigrams), 2 (bigrams), or 3 (trigrams). Higher ROUGE scores indicate a greater overlap between the summary and the original text.
- BLEU (Bilingual Evaluation Understudy) measures the overlap between the summary and the original text in terms of n-grams, where n can be 1 (unigrams), 2 (bigrams), 3 (trigrams), or 4 (4-grams). BLEU is often used to evaluate machine-generated translations, but it can also be used to evaluate summaries.
- The F1 score is a measure of the balance between precision and recall. In the context of summarization, precision measures the proportion of the summary that is relevant to the original text, while recall measures the proportion of the original text that is captured in summary.

Here is an example of how to compute the ROUGE-1, ROUGE-2, and ROUGE-L scores for a summary and the original text in Python:

```python
from rouge import Rouge

# original text
text = "This is a long piece of text that we want to summarize. It includes a variety of information
and ideas, and we want to condense it into a shorter, more concise summary. Extractive summarization
involves selecting key phrases and sentences from the original text, and piecing them together to
create a summary. This can be done manually or automatically using algorithms and natural language
processing techniques. Abstractive summarization, on the other hand, involves generating a summary that
is not directly based on the original text, and requires a more in-depth understanding of the text. It
often involves the use of natural language processing techniques to generate a summary that is more
coherent and reads like a human-written summary."

# summary
summary = "Abstractive summarization involves generating a summary that is not based on the original
text and requires a deeper understanding of the text. Extractive summarization involves selecting key
phrases and sentences from the original text."

# compute ROUGE scores
rouge = Rouge()
scores = rouge.get_scores(summary, text)

# print ROUGE-1, ROUGE-2, and ROUGE-L scores
print(f"ROUGE-1: {scores[0]['rouge-1']['f']}")
print(f"ROUGE-2: {scores[0]['rouge-2']['f']}")
print(f"ROUGE-L: {scores[0]['rouge-l']['f']}")
```

This code will use the Rouge library to compute the ROUGE-1, ROUGE-2, and ROUGE-L scores for the summary and the original text. The ROUGE-1 score measures the overlap in terms of unigrams, the ROUGE-2 score measures the overlap in terms of bigrams, and the ROUGE-L score measures the overlap in terms of the longest common subsequence.

Here is an example of how to implement the BLEU (Bilingual Evaluation Understudy) evaluation metric for text summarization in Python:

```python
from nltk.translate.bleu_score import sentence_bleu

# original text
text = "This is a long piece of text that we want to summarize. It includes a variety of information
and ideas, and we want to condense it into a shorter, more concise summary. Extractive summarization
involves selecting key phrases and sentences from the original text, and piecing them together to
create a summary. This can be done manually or automatically using algorithms and natural language
processing techniques. Abstractive summarization, on the other hand, involves generating a summary that
is not directly based on the original text, and requires a more in-depth understanding of the text. It
often involves the use of natural language processing techniques to generate a summary that is more
coherent and reads like a human-written summary."

# summary
summary = "Abstractive summarization involves generating a summary that is not based on the original
text and requires a deeper understanding of the text. Extractive summarization involves selecting key
phrases and sentences from the original text."

# split text into sentences
text_sentences = text.split('. ')

# compute BLEU score
bleu_score = sentence_bleu(text_sentences, summary)
print(f"BLEU score: {bleu_score}")
```

This code will use the NLTK library to compute the BLEU score for the summary and the original text. The BLEU score measures the overlap between the summary and the original text in terms of n-grams, where n can be 1 (unigrams), 2 (bigrams), 3 (trigrams), or 4 (4-grams). A higher BLEU score indicates a greater overlap between the summary and the original text.

Note that the BLEU score is typically computed using a reference summary rather than the original text, as the reference summary is considered to be a more accurate representation of what a human-written summary would look like. In the example above, we have used the original text as the reference, but in practice, it is generally recommended to use a reference summary when computing the BLEU score.

Here is an example of how to implement the F1 score evaluation metric for text summarization in Python:

```
from sklearn.metrics import f1_score

# original text
text = "This is a long piece of text that we want to summarize. It includes a variety of information
and ideas, and we want to condense it into a shorter, more concise summary. Extractive summarization
involves selecting key phrases and sentences from the original text, and piecing them together to
create a summary. This can be done manually or automatically using algorithms and natural language
processing techniques. Abstractive summarization, on the other hand, involves generating a summary that
is not directly based on the original text, and requires a more in-depth understanding of the text. It
often involves the use of natural language processing techniques to generate a summary that is more
coherent and reads like a human-written summary."

# summary
summary = "Abstractive summarization involves generating a summary that is not based on the original
text and requires a deeper understanding of the text. Extractive summarization involves selecting key
phrases and sentences from the original text."

# split text into sentences
text_sentences = text.split('. ')

# compute F1 score
f1 = f1_score(text_sentences, summary, average='micro')
print(f"F1 score: {f1}")
```

This code will use the sci-kit-learn library to compute the F1 score for the summary and the original text. The F1 score is a measure of the balance between precision and recall. In the context of summarization, precision measures the proportion of the summary that is relevant to the original text, while recall measures the proportion of the original text that is captured in summary. A higher F1 score indicates a greater balance between precision and recall.

Note that this implementation of the F1 score may not be the most appropriate for evaluating text summaries, as it is based on the assumption that each sentence in the text is a separate class.

Sentiment Analysis: Identifying and analysing emotions in text data

CHAPTER
11

Introduction to sentiment analysis

Sentiment analysis, also known as opinion mining, is a subfield of natural language processing (NLP) that aims to identify and extract subjective information from text data. This includes identifying emotions, attitudes, and opinions expressed in the text.

Sentiment analysis is commonly used in a variety of fields, including marketing, customer service, and politics, to better understand the sentiments of customers or constituents. For example, a company may use sentiment analysis to track customer satisfaction with their products or services, or a political campaign may use sentiment analysis to gauge public opinion on a particular issue.

Practical Examples of Sentiment Analysis

- Social media analysis
  One common application of sentiment analysis is analyzing social media posts to understand how people feel about a particular topic or brand. For example, a company may use sentiment analysis to track how its brand is perceived on social media and identify any potential issues that may need to be addressed.

- Customer service
  Sentiment analysis can also be used in customer service to track customer satisfaction and identify any issues that may need to be addressed. For example, a company may use sentiment analysis to analyze customer

reviews or survey responses to understand how customers feel about their products or services.

- **Market research**
  Sentiment analysis can be useful in market research, as it can help companies understand how consumers feel about their products or services, as well as their competitors. This can be particularly useful for tracking trends and identifying potential areas for improvement.

- **Political analysis**
  Sentiment analysis can be used in political analysis to understand public opinion on a particular candidate or issue. For example, a campaign may use sentiment analysis to track how their candidate is perceived on social media or in the news and identify any potential issues that may need to be addressed.

- **Disaster response**
  Sentiment analysis can also be used in disaster response to track public sentiment and identify potential issues that may need to be addressed. For example, during a natural disaster, sentiment analysis may be used to track how people are feeling and identify any potential needs or concerns that may need to be addressed.

Sentiment lexicons and machine learning approaches

Sentiment analysis can be performed using a variety of techniques, including lexicon-based approaches and machine-learning algorithms.

Sentiment lexicons

A sentiment lexicon is a list of words or phrases that are annotated with a sentiment label, such as positive, negative, or neutral. These lexicons can be used to classify the sentiment of a given piece of text by counting the number of positive, negative, and neutral words in the text and determining the overall sentiment based on the majority of the words.

One example of a sentiment lexicon is the AFINN lexicon, which is a list of English words annotated with a sentiment score ranging from 5 (very negative) to 5 (very positive). Another example is the SentiWordNet lexicon, which is a list of English words and phrases annotated with a positive and negative sentiment score.

There are several advantages to using sentiment lexicons, including the fact that they are easy to use and require minimal training data. However, they do have some limitations, including the fact that they are limited to the words and phrases in the lexicon and may not accurately capture the sentiment of words or phrases that are not included in the lexicon.

To use the AFINN lexicon in Python, we can first download the lexicon from the following URL:

https://github.com/fnielsen/afinn/blob/master/afinn/data/AFINN-en-165.txt

Next, we can read the lexicon and create a dictionary mapping each word to its corresponding sentiment score:

```python
import re

afinn_lexicon = {}

with open('AFINN-en-165.txt', 'r') as f:
    for line in f:
        word, score = line.split()
        afinn_lexicon[word] = int(score)
```

We can then use the AFINN lexicon to classify the sentiment of a given piece of text by counting the number of positive and negative words and determining the overall sentiment based on the majority of the words. For example, the following code counts the number of positive and negative words in a given text and determines the overall sentiment based on the majority of the words:

```python
def classify_sentiment(text):
    # Split the text into words
    words = re.findall(r'\w+', text)

    # Initialize counters for positive and negative words
    positive_words = 0
    negative_words = 0

    # Iterate over the words in the text
    for word in words:
        # Check if the word is in the AFINN lexicon
        if word in afinn_lexicon:
            # Increment the appropriate counter based on the sentiment of the word
            if afinn_lexicon[word] > 0:
                positive_words += 1
            else:
                negative_words += 1
```

```
    # Determine the overall sentiment based on the majority of the words
    if positive_words > negative_words:
        return 'positive'
    elif negative_words > positive_words:
        return 'negative'
    else:
        return 'neutral'

# Test the classify_sentiment function
text = 'This is a great product!'
sentiment = classify_sentiment(text)
print(f'The sentiment of the text is {sentiment}.')

text = 'This product is terrible!'
sentiment = classify_sentiment(text)
print(f'The sentiment of the text is {sentiment}.')

text = 'I am not sure if I like this product.'
sentiment = classify_sentiment(text)
print(f'The sentiment of the text is {sentiment}.')
```

The output is shown below:

```
The sentiment of the text is positive.
The sentiment of the text is negative.
The sentiment of the text is neutral.
```

Machine learning approaches

In contrast to lexicon-based approaches, machine learning algorithms can be used to learn the sentiment of a given piece of text from a training dataset. This requires a large dataset of text that has been annotated with sentiment labels, which can be used to train the machine learning model.

There are several machine learning algorithms that can be used for sentiment analysis, including support vector machines (SVMs), random forests, and deep neural networks. These algorithms can be trained to classify the sentiment of a given piece of text based on the words and phrases in the text, as well as other features such as the presence of certain punctuation or the use of certain words.

One advantage of machine learning approaches is that they can often achieve higher accuracy than lexicon-based approaches, as they are able to take into account more context and features of the text. However, they require a large dataset of annotated text for training and may not perform as well on small datasets or texts that are significantly different from the training data.

In this example, we will use a simple logistic regression model, which is a type of linear model that can be used for classification tasks.

To use a logistic regression model for sentiment analysis in Python, we will first need to install the sci-kit-learn library, which provides a range of machine-learning algorithms, including logistic regression. We can install scikit-learn using the following command:

```
pip install scikit-learn
```

Next, we will need to load and prepare a dataset of text that has been annotated with sentiment labels. There are several datasets available for sentiment analysis, including the IMDB movie review dataset and the Stanford Sentiment Treebank dataset. In this example, we will use the IMDB movie review dataset, which consists of 50,000 movie reviews labelled as positive or negative.

We can load and prepare the IMDB movie review dataset using the following code:

```
from sklearn.datasets import load_files

# Load the IMDB movie review dataset
reviews_train = load_files('acllmdb/train/')
reviews_test = load_files('acllmdb/test/')

# Extract the text and labels from the training and test sets
X_train, y_train = reviews_train.data, reviews_train.target
X_test, y_test = reviews_test.data, reviews_test.target
```

The text data is stored in the **X_train** and **X_test** variables, and the labels are stored in the **y_train** and **y_test** variables. The labels are integers representing the sentiment of the text, with 0 representing a negative sentiment and one representing a positive sentiment.

Next, we will need to preprocess the text data by converting it to a numerical format that can be used by the machine learning model. One way to do this is by using a bag-of-words model, which represents each text as a fixed-length vector of the frequency of each word in the text. We can create a bag-of-words model using the **CountVectorizer** class from scikit-learn:

```
from sklearn.feature_extraction.text import CountVectorizer

# Create a bag-of-words model
vectorizer = CountVectorizer(max_features=3000)
X_train_vectors = vectorizer.fit_transform(X_train)
X_test_vectors = vectorizer.transform(X_test)
```

The **CountVectorizer** class takes a parameter **max_features,** which specifies the maximum number of features (i.e., words) to keep based on term frequency.

In this case, we are keeping the 3000 most common words in the dataset.

Finally, we can train a logistic regression model using the preprocessed text data and labels:

```
from sklearn.linear_model import LogisticRegression

# Train a logistic regression model
model = LogisticRegression(max_iter=5000)
model.fit(X_train_vectors, y_train)
```

Once the model is trained, we can evaluate its performance on the test set using the **score** method:

```
# Evaluate the model on the test set
accuracy = model.score(X_test_vectors, y_test)
print(f'Test set accuracy: {accuracy:.2f}')
```

The output of this code should be the accuracy of the model on the test set, which should be around 85-90%, depending on the specific run.

Evaluation metrics for sentiment analysis

When evaluating the performance of a sentiment analysis model, it is important to use appropriate evaluation metrics that accurately reflect the quality of the model's predictions. In this section, we will explore some common evaluation metrics used for sentiment analysis in Python.

Accuracy

Accuracy is perhaps the most intuitive evaluation metric for sentiment analysis, as it measures the proportion of correct predictions made by the model. In other words, it is the percentage of texts that are correctly classified as positive, negative, or neutral.

To calculate accuracy in Python, we can use the **accuracy_score** function from the scikit-learn library:

```
from sklearn.metrics import accuracy_score

# Calculate accuracy
accuracy = accuracy_score(y_true, y_pred)
print(f'Accuracy: {accuracy:.2f}')
```

Where **y_true** is a list of the true labels for each text, and **y_pred** is a list of the predicted labels for each text. The output is the accuracy of the model, which is a value between 0 and 1.

However, it is important to note that accuracy can be misleading when the classes are imbalanced, meaning that one class (e.g., positive sentiment) is much more common than the other class (e.g., negative sentiment). In such cases, a model could achieve high accuracy by simply predicting the majority class all the time, even if it is not very good at detecting the minority class.

Confusion matrix

A confusion matrix is a table that shows the number of true positive, true negative, false positive, and false negative predictions made by the model. It can be helpful in understanding the strengths and weaknesses of a model, as well as identifying any patterns in the errors made by the model.

To create a confusion matrix in Python, we can use the **confusion_matrix** function from the scikit-learn library:

```
from sklearn.metrics import confusion_matrix

# Calculate the confusion matrix
cm = confusion_matrix(y_true, y_pred)
print(cm)
```

Here **y_true** is a list of the true labels for each text, and **y_pred** is a list of the predicted labels for each text. The output is a two-dimensional array, with the rows representing the true labels and the columns representing the predicted labels. For example, in a binary classification task with positive and negative labels, the confusion matrix might look like this:

```
[[True Negative, False Positive]
 [False Negative, True Positive]]
```

Precision and recall

Precision and recall are evaluation metrics used to measure the quality of a model's predictions. Precision measures the proportion of positive predictions that are actually positive, while recall measures the proportion of actual positive cases that were correctly predicted by the model.

To calculate precision and recall in Python, we can use the **precision_score** and **recall_score** functions from the scikit-learn library:

```python
from sklearn.metrics import precision_score, recall_score

# Calculate precision
precision = precision_score(y_true, y_pred)
print(f'Precision: {precision:.2f}')

# Calculate recall
recall = recall_score(y_true, y_pred)
print(f'Recall: {recall:.2f}')
```

Where **y_true** is a list of the true labels for each text, and **y_pred** is a list of the predicted labels for each text. The output is the precision and recall of the model, which are values between 0 and 1.

It is important to note that precision and recall are often in trade-off with each other, meaning that increasing one may decrease the other. For example, a model with high precision may have a low recall and vice versa.

F1 Score

The F1 score is a metric that combines precision and recalls into a single score, which can be helpful for comparing the performance of different models. The F1 score is defined as the harmonic mean of precision and recall.

To calculate the F1 score in Python, we can use the **f1_score** function from the scikit-learn library:

```python
from sklearn.metrics import f1_score

# Calculate F1 score
f1 = f1_score(y_true, y_pred)
print(f'F1 score: {f1:.2f}')
```

Where **y_true** is a list of the true labels for each text, and **y_pred** is a list of the predicted labels for each text. The output is the F1 score of the model, which is a value between 0 and 1.

Advanced NLP Techniques: Deep learning and beyond

CHAPTER 12

Introduction to deep learning in NLP

Deep learning is a type of machine learning that involves the use of neural networks with multiple layers to learn and represent data in a hierarchical manner. These networks are able to automatically learn and extract features from raw input data, making them particularly well-suited for tasks that require understanding and processing complex and unstructured data such as text.

Deep learning has revolutionized the field of natural language processing (NLP) in recent years, leading to significant improvements in tasks such as language translation, sentiment analysis, and text generation.

One of the key benefits of deep learning in NLP is its ability to handle large amounts of data. Traditional NLP approaches often rely on hand-crafted features and rules, which can be time-consuming and error-prone to develop and maintain. Deep learning, on the other hand, can learn directly from raw data and improve its performance as it is exposed to more data.

History of deep learning in NLP

Deep learning in NLP has a long and storied history dating back to the 1950s when researchers first began exploring the use of artificial neural networks for language processing tasks. One of the earliest examples of this was the work of Warren McCulloch and Walter Pitts, who published a paper in 1943 describing a model of the neuron as a simple logical gate.

In the 1950s and 1960s, researchers continued to build on this foundation and develop more sophisticated neural network models for NLP tasks.

However, these early approaches were limited by the computing power available at the time and were often outperformed by traditional rule-based systems.

It wasn't until the late 1980s and early 1990s that deep learning approaches began to gain traction in NLP, with the development of techniques such as backpropagation and the long short-term memory (LSTM) network. These approaches were able to overcome some of the limitations of earlier neural network models and achieved improved results on tasks such as language modelling and machine translation.

The field of deep learning in NLP received a major boost in the late 2000s with the availability of large amounts of labelled data and the development of more powerful computing hardware. This led to the emergence of new deep learning techniques such as word2vec and the convolutional neural network (CNN), which have been widely used in a variety of NLP tasks.

In recent years, transformer models have emerged as a state-of-the-art approach for NLP tasks, achieving impressive results on tasks such as language translation and language modelling. These models are based on the transformer architecture, which uses self-attention mechanisms to process the input data in a parallel rather than in a sequential manner.

Overall, deep learning has revolutionized the field of NLP and has led to significant improvements in tasks such as language translation, sentiment analysis, and text generation. It is now an integral part of the NLP landscape and continues to be an active area of research and development.

Popular deep learning models for NLP

In the following sections, we will cover several popular deep-learning techniques in NLP and provide examples of how they can be applied in practice.

- **Word Embeddings**

  Word embeddings are a way to represent words in a continuous vector space, allowing them to be processed by machine learning algorithms. One of the most popular techniques for creating word embeddings is word2vec, which uses a shallow neural network to learn the relationships between words in a dataset.

  For example, word2vec might learn that the word "king" is often used in the same context as the word "queen"; therefore, the vectors for these words should be similar. This allows the model to understand the meaning of words and their relationships to one another, even if it has never seen them before.

Word embeddings can be used in a variety of NLP tasks, including language translation, text classification, and information retrieval.

- **Recurrent Neural Networks (RNNs)**

  Recurrent neural networks (RNNs) are a type of deep learning model that is particularly well-suited for processing sequential data such as text. RNNs are able to maintain a state that can depend on the previous inputs, allowing them to consider the context of a word within a sentence or document.

  One popular variant of RNNs is the long short-term memory (LSTM) network, which is able to handle long-term dependencies and prevent the vanishing gradient problem that can occur with traditional RNNs. LSTMs have been used successfully in tasks such as language translation, language modelling, and text generation.

- **Convolutional Neural Networks (CNNs)**

  Convolutional neural networks (CNNs) are a type of deep learning model commonly used in image and video recognition tasks. However, they can also be applied to NLP tasks such as text classification and sentiment analysis.

  CNN work by applying a series of filters to the input data to extract local features and patterns. In the case of text classification, the input data could be a sequence of words, and the filters could be designed to identify specific words or combinations of words that are indicative of a particular class.

- **Transformer Models**

  Transformer models are a type of deep learning model that has achieved state-of-the-art results on a variety of NLP tasks, such as language translation and language modelling. They are based on the transformer architecture, which uses self-attention mechanisms to process the input data in a parallel rather than in a sequential manner.

  Transformer models have several advantages over traditional RNN and LSTM models, including the ability to process long sequences of data efficiently, the ability to handle variable-length input sequences, and the ability to parallelize the computation of the self-attention mechanisms.

One popular variant of transformer models is the BERT (Bidirectional Encoder Representations from Transformers) model, which has been used for tasks such as language translation, question answering, and text classification.

Summary of transformer model

The transformer is a neural network architecture for natural language processing tasks that was introduced in the "Attention is All You Need" paper. It is based on the idea of self-attention, which allows the model to directly attend to different parts of the input sequence and incorporate this information into the output.

The transformer model consists of multiple encoder and decoder layers, each of which is composed of self-attention and fully connected layers. The self-attention layers perform a weighted sum of the input data based on a dot product of the input data and a set of learned weights, which allows the model to attend to different parts of the input sequence and incorporate this information into the output.

The transformer model also introduces the concept of multi-head attention, which allows the model to attend to multiple parts of the input simultaneously. This is achieved by performing self-attention with multiple sets of weights in parallel and then concatenating the resulting output.

The transformer model also uses position encoding, which explicitly incorporates the order of the input sequence into the model. This is done by adding a fixed encoding to the input data based on the position of each element in the sequence, which allows the model to learn the relative position of the input elements.

Overall, the transformer model is able to process input data in parallel, which allows it to achieve improved performance and faster training times compared to traditional models such as RNNs and LSTMs. It has become a widely-used approach for a variety of natural language processing tasks and has achieved state-of-the-art results on tasks such as language translation and language modelling.

GPT-3

GPT-3 (Generative Pre-trained Transformer 3) is a large language model developed by OpenAI. It is based on transformer architecture, which is a neural network architecture that has been successful in a wide range of natural language processing tasks.

At a high level, GPT-3 works by taking in a sequence of input text and generating a sequence of output text based on the input. The input and output sequences can be of variable lengths, allowing GPT-3 to be used for tasks such as translation, text generation, and question-answering.

GPT-3 is pre-trained on a massive dataset of web text, which allows it to generate human-like text for a wide range of tasks. The pre-training process involves training the model on a large dataset of text and optimizing it to predict the next word in a sequence given the previous words. This allows the model to learn the statistical patterns and relationships present in the training data, which it can then use to generate coherent and natural-sounding text.

After the pre-training process is complete, GPT-3 can be fine-tuned for specific tasks. This involves adapting the model to a specific task by adjusting its weights and biases to optimize its performance on that task. For example, if GPT-3 is being fine-tuned for translation, it would be trained on a dataset of the translated text and optimized to accurately translate new input text.

GPT-3 has achieved impressive results and has been used for a wide range of tasks, including chatbots and virtual assistants, text generation, translation, and question-answering. It has also garnered significant attention in the field of artificial intelligence and has raised concerns about the potential for it to be used for nefarious purposes, such as the generation of fake news or spam.

Overall, GPT-3 is a powerful and versatile tool for natural language processing tasks, but it is important to consider the ethical implications of its use and ensure that it is used responsibly.

ChatGPT

ChatGPT is a variant of the GPT-3 (Generative Pre-trained Transformer 3) language model that has been specifically designed for use in chatbots and virtual assistants. It is based on transformer architecture, which is a neural network architecture that has been successful in a wide range of natural language processing tasks.

At a high level, ChatGPT works by taking in a sequence of input text and generating a sequence of output text based on the input. The input and output sequences can be of
variable lengths, allowing ChatGPT to be used for tasks such as translation, text generation, and question answering.

ChatGPT is pre-trained on a massive dataset of web text, which allows it to generate human-like text for a wide range of tasks. The pre-training process involves training the model on a large dataset of text and optimizing it to predict the next word in a sequence given the previous words. This allows the model to learn the statistical patterns and relationships present in the training data, which it can then use to generate coherent and natural-sounding text.

After the pre-training process is complete, ChatGPT can be fine-tuned for specific tasks. This involves adapting the model to a specific task by adjusting its weights and biases to optimize its performance on that task. For example, if ChatGPT is being fine-tuned for use in a chatbot, it would be trained on a dataset of conversations and optimized to accurately respond to new input text.

One of the key advantages of ChatGPT is its ability to handle open-ended conversations and respond appropriately to a wide range of inputs. It can also learn from its interactions with users, allowing it to improve over time and adapt to the needs and preferences of individual users.

Overall, ChatGPT is a powerful and versatile tool for natural language processing tasks, and it is particularly well-suited for use in chatbots and virtual assistants.

Advanced NLP applications and future directions

Deep learning has emerged as a powerful tool for NLP tasks and has led to significant improvements in areas such as language translation, sentiment analysis, and text generation. In this section, we will explore some of the advanced NLP applications that are enabled by deep learning, as well as the future directions in which the field is likely to head.

- **Chatbots and Virtual Assistants**
  Chatbots and virtual assistants are computer programs that are able to communicate with users in natural language and perform a variety of tasks, such as answering questions, making recommendations, and scheduling appointments.

  Deep learning approaches, particularly transformer models, have been applied to the development of chatbots and virtual assistants and have achieved impressive results. For example, OpenAI's GPT-3 (Generative Pre-trained Transformer 3) is a transformer-based language model that can generate human-like text for a variety of tasks, such as translation, question answering, and text summarization.

- **Text Summarization**
  Text summarization is the task of generating a summary of a longer piece of text that captures the main points and ideas.

Deep learning approaches, particularly transformer models, have been applied to this task and have achieved impressive results.

For example, OpenAI's GPT-3 can be used to generate summaries of news articles, allowing readers to quickly get up to speed on the latest developments in a particular topic. This could be particularly useful for busy professionals who don't have the time to read through long articles in their entirety.

- **Language Generation**
  Language generation is the task of generating new text that is coherent and coherent with a given prompt or topic. Deep learning approaches, particularly transformer models, have been applied to this task and have produced impressive results.

  For example, OpenAI's GPT-3 can be used to generate human-like text for a variety of tasks, such as translation, question answering, and text summarization. This could be used to automate the creation of content such as news articles, social media posts, or marketing materials.

- **Sentiment Analysis**
  Sentiment analysis is the task of determining the sentiment (positive, negative, or neutral) of a piece of text. Deep learning approaches have been applied to this task using techniques such as word embeddings and CNNs.

  For example, a sentiment analysis model might be trained on a large dataset of movie reviews labelled with their corresponding sentiment. The model could then be used to classify the sentiment of new movie reviews as they come in, allowing a movie studio to gauge the public's response to a new release.

Future Directions in NLP

- **Integration with Other Fields**
  One of the future directions in which NLP is likely to head is the integration with other fields, such as computer vision and robotics. This could enable the development of more sophisticated AI systems that are able to understand and respond to complex environments and tasks.

  For example, a robot equipped with NLP capabilities could be used to navigate and interact with people in a crowded public space, using language understanding and generation to communicate with its surroundings.

- **Continued Improvement in Language Translation**
  Language translation is an area in which deep learning approaches have already achieved impressive results, but there is still room for improvement. In the future, we are likely to see continued advances in this area, including the development of more accurate and efficient translation systems that can handle a wider range of languages and dialects.

- **Personalization and Customization**
  Another direction in which NLP is likely to head is the development of personalized and customized AI systems that are able to adapt to the needs and preferences of individual users. This could involve the use of techniques such as reinforcement learning to optimize the performance of NLP systems based on feedback from users.

- **Increased Use of Pre-trained Models**
  Pre-trained models are machine learning models that have been trained on large amounts of data and can then be fine-tuned for specific tasks. In the future, we are likely to see an increased use of pre-trained models in NLP, as they can save time and resources and allow developers to focus on the specific tasks they are trying to solve.

  In conclusion, NLP is an active and rapidly evolving field with a bright future ahead. Deep learning approaches have already achieved impressive results in areas such as language translation, sentiment analysis, and text generation, and there is still much more to come. The future of NLP is likely to involve integration with other fields, continued improvement in language translation, personalization and customization, and the increased use of pre-trained models.

Real-World Examples

Chatbot Implementation Using GPT-3

A chatbot is a computer program designed to simulate conversation with human users, especially over the Internet. Chatbots can be used in a variety of contexts, such as customer service, entertainment, and information gathering.

One common use case for chatbots is in customer service. Many companies have implemented chatbots on their websites or messaging apps to help answer frequently asked questions and assist customers with common issues. For example, a chatbot might be able to provide a customer with information about their order status, shipping options, or return policy. Chatbots can also be used to help customers troubleshoot technical issues or provide product recommendations.

Another use case for chatbots is in the entertainment industry. Chatbots can be used to create interactive games or chat-based experiences for users. For example, a chatbot might be used to power a trivia game or a choose-your-own-adventure-style story. In these cases, the chatbot is able to understand and respond to user input in real time, providing a more immersive and interactive experience.

In addition to customer service and entertainment, chatbots are also being used in a variety of other contexts. For example, chatbots can be used in healthcare to provide patients with information about their treatment plans or to remind them to take their medication. Chatbots can also be used in education to help students learn new subjects or to provide personalized study plans.

There are many different platforms and tools available for building chatbots, ranging from simple chatbot builders to more advanced artificial intelligence platforms. Some popular options include Dialogflow, Botpress, ManyChat, and OpenAI's GPT-3.

To implement a chatbot using OpenAI's GPT-3 (Generative Pre-trained Transformer 3) model with Python, you will need to follow these steps:

- Sign up for an OpenAI API key: In order to use GPT-3, you will need to sign up for an OpenAI API key. This will allow you to access the GPT-3 API and use it to build your chatbot.
- Install the OpenAI Python library: You will need to install the OpenAI Python library in order to access the GPT-3 API from your Python code. You can do this by running the following command:

```
pip install openai
```

- Choose a GPT-3 model: GPT-3 comes in a variety of sizes, ranging from small to large, with each size offering different capabilities and performance characteristics. You will need to choose the size of the model that is appropriate for your chatbot based on your needs and budget.
- Write code to send requests to the GPT-3 API: Once you have your API key and have installed the OpenAI Python library, you can use the following code to send a request to the GPT-3 API and receive a response:

```
import openai

openai.api_key = "YOUR_API_KEY"

prompt = "What is the weather like today?"

model_engine = "davinci"

completions = openai.Completion.create(engine=model_engine, prompt=prompt,
max_tokens=1024, n=1,stop=None,temperature=0.5)

message = completions.choices[0].text
print(message)
```

This code sends a request to the GPT-3 API with a prompt, which is the text that you want the chatbot to respond to and receives a response in the form of text generated by the GPT-3 model.

- Integrate the chatbot into your application: Once you have the chatbot working, you can integrate it into your application by sending the user's input to the chatbot and displaying the chatbot's response. This can be done using a variety of techniques depending on your specific application.

  Here is an example of how you could integrate the chatbot into a simple command-line application:

```python
import openai

openai.api_key = "YOUR_API_KEY"

model_engine = "davinci"

while True:
    prompt = input("What would you like to ask the chatbot? ")
    completions = openai.Completion.create(engine=model_engine, prompt=prompt,
max_tokens=1024, n=1,stop=None,temperature=0.5)
    message = completions.choices[0].text
    print(message)
```

This code will prompt the user for input, send the input to the chatbot using the GPT-3 API, and then display the chatbot's response.

Fake news detection

Fake news detection is a significant problem that has become more prevalent in recent years with the proliferation of social media and the ease of spreading information online. It is important to be able to identify fake news to protect against the spread of misinformation and to maintain the integrity of news sources.

One approach to detecting fake news is to use machine learning. Machine learning algorithms can analyze patterns in data to identify fake news with a high degree of accuracy. There are several different approaches that can be taken to implement a fake news detection system using machine learning.

One common approach is to use natural language processing (NLP) techniques to analyze the text of a news article. This can involve techniques such as sentiment analysis, which can help identify the overall sentiment of an article, and named entity recognition, which can help identify key entities mentioned in the article.

Another approach is to use machine learning to analyze the structure of the article itself. This can include analyzing the layout and formatting of the article, as well as the use of images and other multimedia elements.

Here is an example of how you might use machine learning to detect fake news in Python:

```python
# Import necessary libraries
import numpy as np
import pandas as pd
from sklearn.feature_extraction.text import CountVectorizer
from sklearn.model_selection import train_test_split
from sklearn.linear_model import LogisticRegression

# Load the data
df = pd.read_csv('fake_news_data.csv')

# Preprocess the data
X = df['article_text']
y = df['is_fake']

# Split the data into training and test sets
X_train, X_test, y_train, y_test = train_test_split(X, y, test_size=0.33, random_state=42)

# Vectorize the data using a CountVectorizer
vectorizer = CountVectorizer()
X_train_vectors = vectorizer.fit_transform(X_train)
X_test_vectors = vectorizer.transform(X_test)

# Train a Logistic Regression model on the training data
model = LogisticRegression()
model.fit(X_train_vectors, y_train)

# Evaluate the model on the test data
accuracy = model.score(X_test_vectors, y_test)
print('Accuracy:', accuracy)
```

In this example, we first import the necessary libraries, including **numpy, pandas,** and various functions from **sklearn.** We then load the data from a CSV file and preprocess it by splitting it into feature and target variables.

Next, we split the data into training and test sets using **train_test_split** from **sklearn.** We then use a **CountVectorizer** to vectorize the text data, which converts the text into a numerical form that can be input into a machine-learning model.

We then train a logistic regression model on the training data and evaluate its performance on the test data. Finally, we print out the accuracy of the model.

This is just one example of how you might use machine learning to detect fake news. There are many other approaches and techniques that you can use, and the specific approach will depend on the nature of the data and the problem you are trying to solve.

Topic modeling

Topic modelling is a technique in natural language processing (NLP) that helps identify the underlying themes or topics in a text. It is commonly used on large collections of documents, such as news articles, to discover the main topics discussed in them and how those topics relate to each other.

One popular method for topic modelling is Latent Dirichlet Allocation (LDA). LDA is a generative model that assumes each document is a mixture of a fixed number of topics and that each word in the document is drawn from one of those topics.

Here's an example of how you can use Python to implement topic modelling on news data using the Gensim library and online data:

- First, you'll need to fetch the news data from an online source. There are many websites and APIs that provide access to news articles, such as Google News, the New York Times API, and the Guardian API. You'll need to sign up for an API key and read the documentation to learn how to use the API to fetch the new data.
- Once you have the news data, you'll need to preprocess it by cleaning and normalizing the text, removing stop words, and stemming or lemmatizing the words to reduce them to their base forms.
- Next, you'll need to create a dictionary of the words in your text data. A dictionary maps each word to a unique integer id.
- Once you have your dictionary, you can create a bag-of-words representation of your text data. This is simply a list of the word counts for each document, with the words represented by their integer ids.
- Now you can train an LDA model on your bag-of-words representation. You'll need to specify the number of topics you want the model to identify.
- Once the model is trained, you can use it to infer the topics present in each document by calling the model's **get_document_topics**() method. This will return a list of tuples, where each tuple represents a topic and its corresponding weight for the document.

Here's some example code that puts these steps together:

```python
import requests
import gensim
from gensim import corpora

# Fetch the news data from an online source
response = requests.get("http://api.example.com/news", params={"api_key": API_KEY})
news_data = response.json()["articles"]

# Preprocess the text data
texts = [preprocess_text(article["text"]) for article in news_data]

# Create a dictionary of the texts
dictionary = corpora.Dictionary(texts)

# Create a bag-of-words representation of the texts
bow_corpus = [dictionary.doc2bow(text) for text in texts]

# Train an LDA model
lda_model = gensim.models.LdaModel(bow_corpus, num_topics=10, id2word=dictionary)

# Infer the topics for each document
for i, bow in enumerate(bow_corpus):
    print("Document {}:".format(i))
    topics = lda_model.get_document_topics(bow)
    for topic in topics:
        print("Topic {} (weight={:.3f})".format(topic[0], topic[1]))
```

This code fetches the news data from an online source using the **requests** library, preprocesses the text data, and trains an LDA model to identify the topics present in each document.

Article generation using advance NLP

Article generation using advanced NLP techniques involves using artificial intelligence to automatically generate written content. This can be useful for a variety of applications, including content creation for websites, blogs, and social media, as well as automatic summarization of long documents and automated translation.

There are various approaches to generating articles using advanced NLP techniques. One approach is to use language models, who are trained on large datasets of human language and can generate text that is similar to human writing. Another approach is to use machine learning algorithms to classify and generate text based on a given topic or prompt.

To generate articles using advanced NLP techniques, you will need to have access to a suitable language model or machine learning algorithm. There are several models and libraries available that can be used for this purpose, such as GPT-3, BERT, and TensorFlow.

Once you have access to a suitable model or algorithm, you can use it to generate articles by providing a prompt or topic. For example, you can use GPT-3 to generate an article by providing a prompt such as "Write an article on the topic of machine learning". The model will then generate an article based on the prompt.

We will use GPT-3, a state-of-the-art language model developed by OpenAI, to generate articles. To get started, you will need to install the OpenAI API client and obtain an API key. You can sign up for an API key at the OpenAI website. Once you have the API key, you can install the OpenAI API client using pip:

```
pip install openai
```

Next, you need to set the API key as an environment variable. You can do this by adding the following line to your .bashrc or .bash_profile file:

```
export OPENAI_API_KEY="your_api_key"
```

Now, let's create a function to generate an article using the OpenAI API. We will pass a prompt to the function, and it will generate an article based on the prompt. Here is the code for the function:

```python
import openai

def generate_article(prompt):
    model_engine = "text-davinci-002"
    prompt = (f"{prompt}")

    completions = openai.Completion.create(
        engine=model_engine,
        prompt=prompt,
        max_tokens=1024,
        n=1,
        stop=None,
        temperature=0.5,
    )

    message = completions.choices[0].text
    return message
```

Now, let's test the function by generating an article on "machine learning." Here is the code:

```
prompt = "Write an article on the topic of machine learning"
article = generate_article(prompt)
print(article)
```

The output of the above code should be a well-written article on the topic of machine learning.

That's it! You have successfully implemented article generation using advanced NLP techniques and open-source models in Python. You can use this technique to generate articles on any topic by providing a prompt to the function.

Semantic-based search

Semantic-based search is a technique used to improve the accuracy and relevance of search results by taking into account the context and meaning of the search query. This type of search is particularly useful for natural language queries, where the user may not use the exact keywords or phrases that are present in the documents being searched.

To implement a semantic-based search, we can use various NLP (Natural Language Processing) techniques to extract the meaning and context of the search query and compare it with the contents of the documents being searched.

One approach is to use word embeddings, which are mathematical representations of words in a vector space. We can use a pre-trained word embedding model, such as Word2Vec or GloVe, to convert the words in the search query and the documents into numerical vectors. These vectors capture the meaning and context of the words, and we can then use similarity measures, such as cosine similarity, to compare the vectors and rank the documents based on how closely they match the search query.

Here's an example of how we can use the Word2Vec model to perform a semantic-based search in Python:

```python
from gensim.models import Word2Vec
from gensim.similarities import WmdSimilarity

# Load the Word2Vec model
model = Word2Vec.load("word2vec.model")

# Define the search query
query = "What is the capital of France?"

# Tokenize the query and convert it to a list of vectors
query_vectors = [model[word] for word in query.split() if word in model]

# Define the documents to be searched
documents = ["Paris is the capital of France", "The Eiffel Tower is located in Paris"]

# Convert the documents to a list of lists of vectors
doc_vectors = [[model[word] for word in doc.split() if word in model] for doc in documents]

# Create a WmdSimilarity object
index = WmdSimilarity(doc_vectors, model)

# Perform the search and print the results
sims = index[query_vectors]
print(sims)
```

This code will output a list of similarity scores, indicating how closely each document matches the search query. The document with the highest score is the most relevant result.

This is just a simple example of how semantic-based search can be implemented in Python. In a real-world application, you would need to build a larger database of words and their meanings and use more advanced NLP techniques to better understand the context and intent behind the user's search query.

Autocomplete using NLP

Autocomplete is a feature that suggests possible words or phrases based on the input of a user. It is commonly used in search engines and text editors to help users save time and effort by providing options for commonly used words or phrases.

We will go through the implementation of auto-suggestion in Python using the **difflib** library. The **difflib** library is a part of the Python standard library and provides classes and functions for comparing sequences.

The first step is to import the **difflib** library and create a list of words that we want to use for the suggestion. For this purpose, we will use a list of fruit names.

```
import difflib

words = ['apple', 'banana', 'orange', 'mango', 'grapes', 'peach']
```

Next, we will define a function **suggest** that takes in a word as an argument and returns a list of suggested words based on the input word. We will use the **difflib.get_close_matches** function to find the closest matching words from the list of words that we defined earlier.

```
def suggest(word):
    return difflib.get_close_matches(word, words, n=5, cutoff=0.5)
```

The **difflib.get_close_matches** function returns a list of words that match the input word with a certain degree of similarity. The **n** argument specifies the maximum number of suggestions to return, and the **cutoff** argument specifies the minimum similarity required for a word to be considered a suggestion.

Now, let's test our **suggested** function by calling it with different input words.

```
print(suggest('appl'))
# Output: ['apple']

print(suggest('banana'))
# Output: ['banana']

print(suggest('orang'))
# Output: ['orange']

print(suggest('mang'))
# Output: ['mango']

print(suggest('graps'))
# Output: ['grapes']

print(suggest('peah'))
# Output: ['peach']
```

As you can see, the **suggest** function returns the correct suggestions for different input words.

CLOSING THOUGHTS

"In conclusion, '**An Introduction to Natural Language Processing: A Practical Guide for Beginners**' is an excellent resource for anyone looking to gain a foundational understanding of the field of Natural Language Processing (NLP). The book effectively balances theoretical concepts with practical examples, making it a valuable guide for those new to the field.

The organization of the book is excellent for introducing the reader to the various NLP approaches and algorithms, such as tokenization, stemming, and lemmatization.

It also provides clear explanations of how they work and when to apply them. The book also covers more advanced topics, like sentiment analysis, named entity recognition, Transformer, GPT-3, and ChatGPT and provides a glimpse into the current state of the field and its future directions.

One of the strengths of this book is its focus on hands-on learning. The book includes numerous examples and uses cases throughout the book, which allow the reader to immediately apply what they have learned and solidify their understanding of the material. The last chapter of the book includes various real-time use cases (uses and implementation of the real-time use cases), which provide even more opportunities for the reader to practice and experiment with NLP techniques.

The book is well-organized and simple to navigate, and the writing is clear and succinct, making the topic easy to understand. It highlights the real-world applications of NLP, providing examples from various industries, which helps the reader to see the relevance and potential of the field.

Overall, this book provides a comprehensive introduction to NLP and is an excellent starting point for anyone interested in the field. Whether you are a beginner just starting to explore NLP or an experienced professional looking to brush up on your skills, this book is an invaluable resource. It is a must-read for anyone looking to deepen their understanding of NLP and its potential to transform various industries."

AFTERWORD

Thank you for reading **Introduction to Natural Language Processing: A practical guide for beginners!**

If you have any questions, feedback or praise, please reach me at:

hellointroductiontonlpbeginner@gmail.com

You may also connect with me personally.

sakilansari4@gmail.com

https://www.linkedin.com/in/sakilansari

https://twitter.com/SakilAnsari94

https://github.com/Sakil786

I could not end this book without thanking the many amazing people and my friends who have supported me with the book.

Thank you all.

email

linkedin

twitter

github

www.ingramcontent.com/pod-product-compliance
Lightning Source LLC
Chambersburg PA
CBHW040218090326
40690CB00067B/5306